T

Trans P

ACCOMMODATION AND VISITOR GUIDE

GH00373290

EXCELLENT BOOKS

EXCELLENT BOOKS
94 BRADFORD ROAD
WAKEFIELD
WEST YORKSHIRE WF1 2AE
TEL / FAX: (01924) 315147
E-mail: richard@excellentbooks.co.uk
Website: www.excellentbooks.co.uk

First Published January 2001
Second Edition September 2002

ISBN 1-901464-15-6

Whilst the author has cycled and researched the route for the purposes of
this guide, no responsibility can be accepted for any unforeseen circumstances
encountered whilst following it. The publisher would, however, welcome
information regarding any material changes and problems encountered.

Front cover photos, from left to right:
Enjoying a drink at the Wortley Arms Hotel, Wortley
Top - Cyclists on the Longdendale Trail
Bottom - Walker on the Godley-Apethorn railpath
Cyclists and horseriders on the Upper Don Trail
Frontispiece: TPT running alongside River Don near Sprotbrough

Printed in Great Britain by:
FM Repro Ltd.
Repro House, 69 Lumb Lane
Roberttown
Liversedge
West Yorkshire WF15 7NB

CONTENTS

Liverpool waterfront (section 1 - city centre spur)

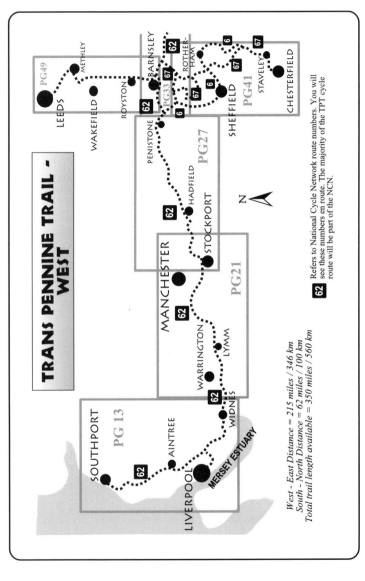

TRANS PENNINE TRAIL - WEST

West - East Distance = 215 miles / 346 km
South - North Distance = 62 miles / 100 km
Total trail length available = 350 miles / 560 km

62 Refers to National Cycle Network route numbers. You will see these numbers en route. The majority of the TPT cycle route will be part of the NCN.

LEEDS
METHLEY
WAKEFIELD
ROYSTON
BARNSLEY
ROTHER-HAM
STAVELEY
CHESTERFIELD
SHEFFIELD
PENISTONE
HADFIELD
STOCKPORT
MANCHESTER
WARRINGTON
LYMM
WIDNES
LIVERPOOL
AINTREE
SOUTHPORT
MERSEY ESTUARY

PG49
PG33
PG41
PG27
PG21
PG13

N

4

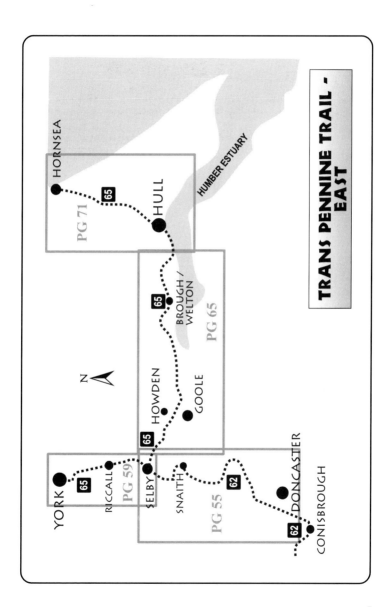

TRANS PENNINE TRAIL - EAST

5

INTRODUCTION

WHAT IS THE TRANS PENNINE TRAIL (TPT)?

• The first multi-user long distance route in the country.
• A recreation and transport route, currently for walkers and cyclists, with sections also available for horse riders and people using wheelchairs and pushchairs.
• A coast to coast route, linking the ports of Liverpool and Hull with connections to the seaside resorts of Southport on the Irish Sea and Hornsea on the North Sea.
• It links major towns and cities across the North including Leeds, Wakefield, Barnsley, York, Selby, Manchester, Doncaster, Rotherham, Sheffield and Chesterfield.
• 215 miles (346km) coast to coast, with a total trail length of 350 miles (560km).
• A very large percentage of the route avoids roads, using disused railway lines, riversides, canal towpaths and cross-country paths.
• Part of the National Cycle Network, which will total more than 10,000 miles by 2005. It links with many other cycle routes including Sustrans' Hull-Fakenham and White Rose routes.
• Developed by a unique partnership of 26 local authorities across the North, with the project office based in Barnsley, South Yorkshire.
• It is the first designated European Long Distance Route for walkers in the country, linking the west of Ireland with Bulgaria and Turkey. (Long distance route E8).

ACCESS, SIGNING AND USER GROUPS

The whole of the TPT is now signed, both ways, and available for use. The full route is for walkers and cyclists with long stretches also for horse riders. Many miles have relatively easy access suitable for some trail users with physical disabilities or families with young children. Efforts will continue beyond 2002 to continually improve and enhance the trail for all users.

FRIENDS OF THE TRANS PENNINE TRAIL

The Friends of the Trans Pennine Trail is a voluntary body of people who want to get the most out of the trail and see it succeed. They help by lobbying and campaigning, practical assistance, supporting the trail project team, promoting the TPT and operating a system of voluntary trail stewards.

For further details contact the Friends' Secretary:

Richie Haynes, 32 Dalebrook Court, Sheffield S10 3PQ (0114) 2305358
e-mail: richard@haynes1.fsnet.co.uk

ROUTE FEATURES - A SUMMARY

Landscape features, west to east:

Formby / Ainsdale Hills - unusual dune landscape, with sands still accumulating as the sea retreats.
Mersey Estuary - Liverpool spur finishes at the Pierhead on the Mersey. The main route comes alongside the Mersey near Widnes, passing beneath the spectacular Runcorn Bridge.
River Mersey South Manchester. Flood plain and gravel pit provide wildlife havens.
Central Pennines - Dark Peak area. Pass down Longdendale, flanked by high, brooding Shining Clough Moss and Highstone Rocks.
East Yorkshire Plain Flat, open countryside, crossed by drainage ditches and punctuated by graceful church spires.
Humber Estuary - Massive! Contains water from a fifth of the country's rivers.

Man-made features, west to east:

Southport Architecture - Beautiful arcades on Lord Street plus recently restored pier and miles of open sand.
Liverpool - Anglican and Roman Catholic cathedrals plus Liver Building.
Manchester Ship Canal - 36 miles long (the route uses only a short section). Little-used by ships nowadays but still spectacular.
Yorkshire's Industrial Heritage - mining site reclamation at the Earth Centre and throughout much of the South and West Yorkshire area.
Conisbrough Castle - Impressive ruins with 90 feet high, 12th century keep.
Magna Award-winning Science Adventure Centre in the former Templeborough steelworks.
Sheffield - former 'steel city', with a small portion of the famous knife blade industry remaining.
Leeds - financial centre of the North, once a centre of the wool trade. Fine Victorian buildings including the Cornmarket, food market and Town Hall. Royal Armouries. Thwaites Mill Industrial Museum on TPT canal section, south of centre.
York - Superlative Minster and rich historical legacy with a wealth of fascinating buildings and outstanding city walls.
Stunningly graceful **Abbeys and Minsters** of East Yorks - e.g. Selby & Howden.
Stunning **Humber Bridge**, with its huge single-span central section.
Hull's Docks Britain's third largest port after London and Liverpool. Infilled docks now form part of city centre. Interesting Old Town area with Maritime Museum and William Wilberforce (anti-slavery campaigner) connections.

SIGNIFICANT TRAFFIC-FREE SECTIONS (Railpath and canal towpath)

TRAIL	FROM	TO	KM	SECT.
Cheshire Lines	Ainsdale	Maghull	16	1
Liverpool Loop Line	Aintree	Halewood	16	1
St Helens Canal	Spike Island	Warrington	10	2
Broadheath - Lymm Railpath	Lymm	Altrincham	14	2
River Mersey Path	Sale	Stockport	15	2
Longdendale Trail	Hadfield Station	Windle Edge	10.5	3
Upper Don	Dunford Bridge	Wortley	17	3
Dove Valley Trail	Silkstone Common	Wombwell	12	4
Five Weirs Walk	Meadowhall	Sheffield	7	5
Beighton - Staveley	Beighton	Staveley	9	5
Chesterfield Canal	Staveley	Chesterfield	8	5
Aire & Calder Navigation	Wood Row Mickletown	Leeds	10	6
York - Selby	Selby	York	24	6
Hull - Hornsea	Hull	Hornsea	21	10

MAPS AND TRANSPORT

Three official map guides show all route options for walkers, cyclists and horse riders. Together with this guide they provide all the information trail users need, along the whole length of the trail. The maps are available separately or as a set from the Trans Pennine Trail Office (see below) or from all good bookshops;

Trans Pennine Trail West Irish Sea to Pennines £4.95 ISBN 0-9532277-1-5
Trans Pennine Trail Central Derbyshire & Yorkshire £4.95 ISBN 0-9532277-2-3
Trans Pennine Trail East Yorkshire to North Sea £4.95 ISBN 0-9532277-3-1

Much of the TPT is well served by rail. The official map guides show railway stations near to the trail. The two main exceptions where train transport becomes more distant are the Longdendale Trail area and the Hull-Hornsea section. Bikes usually cost £3 per trip on inter-city journeys and space must be reserved. For details about carrying bikes on local services ask the local train operating company. A very useful leaflet 'Cycling by train' by Brompton, available from railway stations, describes policy and gives contact details for the different train operating companies. Buses are handy for walkers but will normally only take folding bikes. Details of ferry connections are given in the 'Information File' sections at the end of the relevant chapters.

Please reduce impact on the environment by using public transport to get to the TPT whenever you can. Covering a linear stretch of the route is easier with no need to retrace your steps and you'll be helping to support local services. If you do travel by car, car parks are sparse on many parts of the route. Please be considerate and do not obstruct farm gates or residential access points when you park.

National Train Information 08457 484950 or www.thetrainline.com
Local Travel Information (buses, trains and trams)
Merseyside (0151) 2367676   8 til 8 daily (ferry info as well) www.merseytravel.gov.uk
Greater Manchester (0161) 2287811   7 until 8 daily www.GMPTE.gov.uk
Derbyshire 0870 6082608   7 until 8 daily www.derbysbus.net
South Yorkshire (01709) 515151   7 until 10 daily www.SYPTE.co.uk
West Yorkshire (0113) 2457676   8 until 8 daily www.wymetro.com
East Yorkshire (01482) 222222   (buses only) 8 until 8 daily www.eyms.co.uk

BACKUP PROVIDERS AND HOLIDAY COMPANIES

Holiday Lakeland Provide fully supported holidays along the whole of the TPT including accommodation and luggage transfers. (016973) 71871 **www.holiday-lakeland.co.uk** See ad on page 84 for the full range of services.
Yorkshire Bikelinerare based in Hull and can provide a variety of services along the TPT and further afield, including luggage transfer and motorised backup.
(01482) 222122   **www.bikeliner.karoo.net**
Blue Mountain Hare A small local company based in Shepley just outside Huddersfield offering bespoke activity breaks in the South Pennines/Peak District. Guided or self-guided, specialising in mountain biking, walking and some cycle touring. Frequent use of sections of the Trans Pennine Trail. Bike Hire of top quality mountain bike by prior arrangement. (01484) 603261 **www.bluemountainhare.com**

USEFUL CONTACT ADDRESSES

Trans Pennine Trail Office Barnsley Metropolitan Borough Council, Central Offices, Kendray Street, Barnsley S70 2TN Tel: (01226) 772574
e-mail: transpenninetrail@barnsley.gov.uk   www.transpenninetrail.org.uk
Local Authorities have developed and look after the trail in their area. See phone book or enquire at TPT office for details of relevant local authority.
Friends of the Trans Pennine Trail See page 6.
Ramblers Association Second Floor. Camelford House. 87-90, Albert Embankment, London. SE1 7TW Tel: (020) 73398500 www.ramblers.org.uk
Sustrans 35 King Street, Bristol BS1 4DZ Tel: (0117) 9290888 www.nationalcyclenetwork.org.uk
Cyclists Touring Club Cotterell House, 69 Meadrow, Godalming, Surrey GU7 3HS Tel: 0870 8730061 www.ctc.org.uk
British Horse Society Stoneleigh Deer Park, Kenilworth, Warwickshire CV8 2XZ Tel: (01926) 707700   www.bhs.org.uk
Camping & Caravanning Club Greenfields House, Westwood Way, Coventry CV4 8JH Tel: (024) 76694995 www.campingandcaravanningclub.co.uk
YHA Trevelyan House.Dimple Road, Matlock. Derbyshire DE4 3YH Tel : 0870 870 8808 www.yha.org.uk

Trans Pennine Trail

TRAIL USERS' CODE

The Trans Pennine Trail is a route for walkers, cyclists and horseriders. They often share the same path or occasionally the path is divided for different users. Some sections are not available to horses and some may be difficult for people using wheelchairs or pushchairs though much of the Trail is fully accessible.

To keep everybody safe and happy.....................

Every effort has been made to create a route suitable for all permitted users, but enjoyment of the Trans Pennine Trail relies on everybody showing consideration to each other:

- where different paths, or sides of the path are signed for different user groups - please keep to yours
- if in a group, please do not walk or ride across the whole width of the path, leave space for others to pass you easily
- take great care where the Trans Pennine Trail crosses or follows roads
- take all your litter home and be careful with cigarette ends due to risk of fire

- dog owners - please clean up after your pet - dog mess spoils the trail and adjacent areas for other people and poses health risks
- keep close control of your dog - preferably on a short lead, especially where farm animals are present

- use only sections of the trail where horses are allowed
- do not use the trail unless you can control your horse - you may encounter walkers, people using wheelchairs and scooters, cyclists, dogs and bridges over road, rail and water
- do not canter or gallop on shared sections of the trail
- please avoid damaging trail surfaces and don't ride on the grass central dividing strip

- warn others when you approach from behind so you do not startle people as you pass by - call politely or use a bell / hooter
- slow down when approaching other users who are unpredictable, particularly children or animals. Remember too, some people may be deaf or hard of hearing
- helmets and high visibility clothing will add to your safety
  please ride in single file on narrow sections

- must not use this route for racing competitions or speed trials
- on canal towpaths - read and abide by the British Waterways code for cyclists and only cycle in daylight
- please be prepared to dismount occasionally - on steep access ramps, or on limited sections (such as restricted width bridges)
- where the trail is a designated bridleway, cyclists should give way to other users
- be careful with your speed - especially on slopes or where visibility ahead is limited - do not risk a skid
- Motorbikes are not allowed on the traffic-free sections of the trail.

Everybody - *Please enjoy the Trans Pennine Trail and help others to do so too!*

IMPORTANT

Please note that the route maps shown at the beginning of each chapter throughout this guide are schematic only. For actual user details and navigation on the ground please refer to the official TPT maps detailed on page 8.

1 SOUTHPORT - WIDNES

Section Distance 29 miles / 47km

The Route From Southport head through the beautiful dunes of the Birkdale Hills then inland and onto the Cheshire Lines, through flat market gardening country towards Maghull. Track, canal towpath and minor roads link to the Liverpool Loop Line, like the Cheshire Lines, a disused railway. Out of the Liverpool suburbs you are onto minor roads through pretty Hale village before spectacular off-road sections by the Mersey estuary around the Widnes-Runcorn bridge. Walkers and cyclists are separated for only a very short while, in the dune area south of Southport.

A 7.5 mile spur leads off the Liverpool Loop Line near Childwall. Attractive suburbs and parks lead into Liverpool centre, passing the stunning Anglican Cathedral to finish in the famous dock area with linking ferries to the Isle of Man and Dublin. This uses mainly minor roads and cycle lanes with shared use paths through Sefton and Princes Parks. Full details begin on page 14.

HOTELS & GUESTHOUSES

Carlton Lodge Hotel, 43 Bath Street, Southport PR9 0DP (01704) 542290  www.carltonlodgehotel.co.uk £22-25. ◆◆◆◆ 3s1d6f March-October ✕ **Dist.** 0.75 miles

Edendale Hotel, 83 Avondale Road North, Southport PR9 0NE (01704) 530718 www.edendale-hotel.co.uk £22.50 2s3d1t2f ✕ **Dist.** 0.75 miles

Fairfield Private Hotel, 83 Promenade, Southport PR9 0JN (01704) 530137 £22-27 ◆◆◆ 8 rooms by arrangement **Dist.** 1 mile

Sidbrook Hotel, 14 Talbot Street, Southport PR9 1HP (01704) 530608. sidbrookhotel@tesco.net £22.50. ◆◆◆ 2t 6d **Dist.** 0.5 miles.

Whitworth Falls Hotel, 16 Lathom Road, Southport PR9 0JH (01704) 530074. whitworthfalls@rapid.co.uk / www.whitworthfallshotel.co.uk £19-25 **R** 13 rooms **Dist.** 2 miles Small fee.

There shouldn't be any problem finding accommodation in Southport at short notice outside of the busiest of peak seasons; much of it is on **Bath Street**, **Bold Street** and **Duke Street**.

FOR ACCOMMODATION SYMBOLS KEY SEE INSIDE COVER

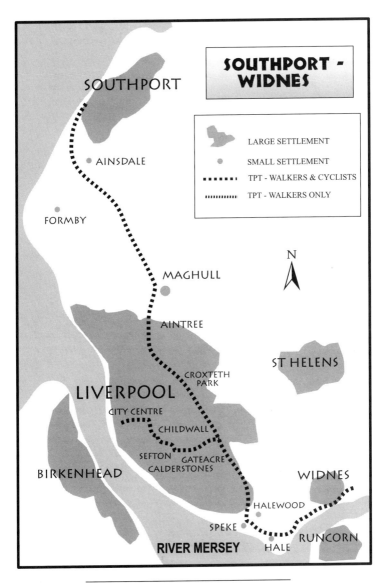

A Church View Guest House, 7 Church Avenue, Aintree, Liverpool L9 4SG (0151) 5258166. £16.♦♦
🛏 3t ⑥ **Dist.** on the route

Parkland, 38 Coachmans Drive, Croxteth Park, Liverpool L12 0HX (0151) 2591417. £20.♦♦♦ 🛏1d1t 🔘 ⬛ ⑥ ✗**Dist.** 1.25 miles

Gateacre Hall Hotel, The Nook, Halewood Road, Gateacre, Liverpool L25 5PG (0151) 4286322 Fax (0151) 4284302. £27-36 (cheaper price applies at weekends) ★★★ 🛏 20d/s 🔘 🔘 ⬛ 🍸 **Dist.** 0.25 miles Residential bar.

Church End Farm, 5 Church End, Hale L24 4AX (0151) 4254273.
🖥churchendfarm@talk21.com £20. **R.** 🛏 2s4d 🔘 ⬛ 🍸 ⑥ ✗
Dist. 0.25 miles

Motel Olympia, Tanhouse Lane, Widnes WA8 0RR (0151) 4246355.
🖥motelolympia@aol.com £17.50. 🛏 23sdt1f 🔘 ⬛ ⑥ Laundry service. **Dist.** 0.75 miles

Mersey Hotel, 147 Mersey Road, West Bank, Widnes WA8 0DT (0151) 4242272
🖥 contact@themerseyhotel1458.greyarcher.org £18.50 🔘 (in season, by arrangement out of season) 🔘 On request 🍸 ⬛ ⑥ Pressure hose for cycle washing. **Dist.** On trail by Widnes-Runcorn bridge.

HOSTELS & CAMPSITES

Willowbank Holiday Home and Touring Park, Coastal Road, Ainsdale, Southport PR8 3ST (01704) 571566. £3.50 per person per night (tents). Open March - early January. Toilets, showers and laundry facilities. Mini-market type shop nearby.

Thatched cottage at Hale, east of Liverpool John Lennon Airport (section 1)

FOOD & DRINK

Plenty of food and drink outlets in **Southport**.
National Wildflower Centre Next to the trail, just before the spur off to the city centre. Toilets and cafe outside of admission paygate. See below for details.
Gateacre Park Drive, just off the Liverpool Loop Line near the link to Liverpool city centre and pier head, has take-aways, restaurants and a nearby pub.
Childe of Hale Pub, 6 Church End, Hale Village. Bar snacks. (0151) 4252954
Wellington pub on TPT in Hale. Hale Post Office sells snacks.

ATTRACTIONS

Southport Elegant seaside resort. Grand architecture on Lord Street.
Attractive **Marine Lake** and **Pier** area front onto miles of open sands.
Museum in Botanic Gardens at Churchtown holds impressive collection of Victoriana (01704) 227547. **Model Railway Village** is a family favourite, recently opened after closure of previous model village (01704) 214266. The **Pier** is one of the longest in the UK and is being restored in phases, the first having been recently completed.
Croxteth Country Park Edwardian country house over 500 acres of parkland. House, home farm and Victorian walled garden. (0151) 2285311. Refreshments / toilets.
National Wildflower Centre, Court Hey Park. Working nursery in 35 acres of open space. Seasonal opening. (0151) 7371819 www.nwc.org.uk
Hale Village inn sign depicts John Middleton, reputed 9ft 3 inch giant who defeated James I's wrestling champion in 17th century. Pretty village with 18th century church. Ruins of Hale Hall to west of village. Unusual 'Childe of Hale', sculptured from a tree stump on road to estuary front and lighthouse.
Pickerings Pasture Local nature reserve with wild flower meadows and views across the River Mersey. Hale Marshes birdwatching area. Ranger centre and toilets.
Widnes Centre of chemical industry. Spectacular views from Widnes-Runcorn Bridge, where St Helens Canal and Manchester Ship Canal join Mersey estuary.

INFORMATION FILE

Tourist Information
Southport: 112 Lord Street (01704) 533333.
Runcorn & Widnes: 6 Church Street, Runcorn (01928) 576776.
Hospital Southport & Formby General, Town Lane, Southport (01704) 547471
Banks All main high street banks in Southport and Widnes centres.
🚲 **Birkdale Cycles** 272 Liverpool Road, Southport (01704) 567351
NE Mosscrop 78 Bispham Road, Southport (01704) 228805
Aintree Bike Centre 336 Longmoor Lane, Aintree, Liverpool (0151) 5217821
Bike King 277 East Prescott Road, Knotty Ash, Liverpool (0151) 4752882
Crays Cycles Ltd 207 Liverpool Road North, Maghull (0151) 5269566
John Geddes Cycles 43 Widnes Road, Widnes (0151) 4207797

HOTELS & GUESTHOUSES - LIVERPOOL CENTRE SPUR

Real McCoy Guesthouse, 126 Childwall Park Avenue, Liverpool L16 0JH (0151) 7227116. From £25. ♦♦♦ 🛌 1s2d 🍽 ⬚ 👕 **Dist.** 0.25 miles

Somersby, 57 Green Lane, Menlove Gardens, Calderstones, Liverpool L18 2EP Tel/fax (0151) 7227549. £19-22.50 ♦♦♦ 🍽 ⬚ 🚲 ✕ **Dist.** 0.25 miles

Blenheim Lodge, 37 Aigburth Drive, Sefton Park, Liverpool L17 4JE (0151) 7277380 Fax (0151) 7275833 ◼theblenheimguesthouse@BTinternet.com £18.50. ♦♦♦ 🛌 16 s/d/f 🍽 🍽 ⬚ 👕 🚲 **Dist.** 0.25 miles. Residential bar.

Solna Hotel, 4 Croxteth Drive,Sefton Park, Liverpool L17 3AD (0151) 7343398 Fax (0151) 7344840 ◼ www.feathers.uk.com £22-29. 🛌 20 rooms 🍽 🍽 🚲 **Dist.** 0.25 miles. Residential bar.

Liverpool University c/o Conference Services, Greenbank Conference Park, Berby & Rathbone Hall, North Mossley Hill Road, Liverpool L18 8BH (0151) 7946440 Fax (0151) 7946520 ◼ conference@liv.ac.uk £15-17 🛌 400 single rooms and 160 self-catering apartments at two campuses. Only available over two periods in spring and summer. Call for more details of exact services and availability dates. **Dist.** Campuses near Sefton Park and city centre.

Aachen Hotel, 89-91 Mount Pleasant, Liverpool L3 5TB (0151) 7093477/ 7093633 Fax (0151) 7091126 £20 ♦♦♦ 🛌 various 🍽 🍽 ⬚ 👕 🚲 Bar games / pool. **Dist.** 0.5 miles from Liverpool spur, near city centre.

HOSTELS & CAMPSITES - LIVERPOOL CENTRE SPUR

YHA Liverpool International, 25 Tabley Street, Off Wapping, Liverpool L1 8EE 0870 7705924 ◼liverpool@yha.org.uk £18.50. 🛌100 beds. Mainly 4-6 bed rooms and 4 doubles (all en-suite) 🍽 🍽 ⬚ 👕 🚲 **Dist.** 0.25 miles. Self-catering facilities.

FOOD & DRINK - LIVERPOOL CENTRE SPUR

Childwall Hotel and Restaurant Good range of beers and reasonably priced food (0151) 7225293. Accommodation also.
Snack bar in centre of **Sefton Park**.
Chinatown, with a good choice of restaurants, approaching Liverpool centre.

Approaching the towering Anglican cathedral in Liverpool (section 1 - centre spur)

ATTRACTIONS - LIVERPOOL CENTRE SPUR

7 miles of docks still line the estuary front of what was once the premier Atlantic port of Europe. Shipping declined,leaving decay in its wake but much of the city has been regenerated. Outstanding cultural, architectural and visitor highlights are:

1. **Anglican Cathedral** Incredible views from 331ft tower. Completed 1904-1978. Stunning building sitting on wooded crag. (0151) 7096271.
2. **Chinatown** Good selection of restaurants.
3. **Roman Catholic Cathedral** Circular building from 1960s. Beautiful lantern tower with stained glass. (0151) 7099222.
4. **St George's Hall** Imposing neo-classical building with luxurious interior. For limited seasonal opening times call (0151) 7072391.
5. **Liverpool Museum & Planetarium** From natural history to outer space. (0151) 4784399.
6. **Albert Dock Area** Numerous attractions in converted warehouse include: **Beatles Story** (0151) 7091963 **Tate Gallery**, largest collection of contemporary art outside London (0151) 7027400 **Merseyside Maritime Museum** showing city's history of sugar and slave trading, White Star and Cunard liner businesses and the vast 19th century emigration via the port (0151) 4784499.
7. **Museum of Liverpool Life** Mersey culture and local people (0151) 4784080.
8. **Mersey Ferries** 50 minute cruise leaving from in front of famous landmark of **Liver Building**. (0151) 2272660.
9. **Western Approaches** Original World War II underground H.Q. 50,000 sq ft of operations rooms. (0151) 2272008.

INFORMATION FILE - LIVERPOOL CENTRE SPUR

Tourist Information Atlantic Pavilion, Albert Dock and also Queen's Square 0906 680 6886 (25p a minute) or (0151) 7095111
Hospital Liverpool Royal Hospital, Prescot Street (0151) 7062000
Banks All main high street banks with cashpoints in central shopping area of Liverpool, just to the north of the TPT route along Lower Duke Street.
Transport Seacat services to Isle of Man and Dublin leave from Prince's landing stage, north of Liver Building,adjacent to Pier Head and Mersey ferry terminal. 08705 523523.
🚲 **Abbey Cycles** 44 Childwall Abbey Road, Childwall, Liverpool (0151) 7220999
Rose Lane Cycles 27 Rose Lane, Mossley Hill, Liverpool (0151) 7245240

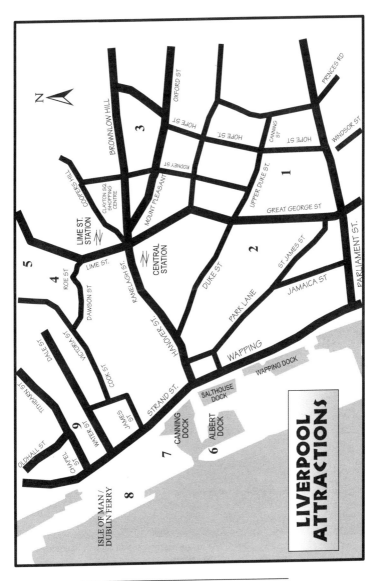

LIVERPOOL ATTRACTIONS

2 WIDNES - STOCKPORT

Section Distance 32miles / 52km

The Route At Widnes you pick up the St. Helens Canal towpath with fine views over the Mersey Estuary where it begins to narrow. Crossing the Mersey south of Warrington leads to a short but spectacular section alongside the Manchester Ship Canal. A 9 mile / 15km section of disused railpath then crosses the Cheshire plain and enters the Trafford district of Greater Manchester. Although this area is often associated with chemicals production the trail largely avoids areas of heavy industry and passes close to such gems as Grappenhall and Lymm. Along the Mersey Valley, south of central Manchester, and through Stockport the route uses a wide-ranging mixture of paths (some alongside the River Mersey) and a variety of roads. Finally you have the option of going through Stockport centre or taking a more northern option towards Hyde. There are several walkers' options along the Mersey Valley section.

HOTELS & GUESTHOUSES

Maples Guesthouse, 11 Longdin Street, Latchford, Warrington WA4 1PW (01925) 637752. £15-20. 1s1d3t1f (by arrangement) **Dist.** 0.5 miles

Imperial Hotel, Bewsey Road, Warrington WA5 0LG (01925) 637255. £16-22-50. 4s1t1tr **Dist.** 1 mile. Breakfast £4.50 extra.

Brook Cottage, Kay Lane, Lymm WA13 0TN (01925) 755530. £25. 2s1t **Dist.** 0.75 miles

Rams Head Pub, Church Lane, Grappenhall Village, Grappenhall, Warrington WA4 3EP (01925) 262814 davidcross1@lineone.net £25 1s2t **Dist.** 0.5 miles. Also see Food & Drink entry.

Bollington Hall Farm, Park Lane, Little Bollington, Altrincham WA14 4TJ (0161) 9281760. £18. **R.** (Notice required) **Dist.** 2.5 miles.

Belvedere Guesthouse, 58 Barrington Road, Altrincham WA14 1HY (0161) 9415996. £19-24. 2d1t1f **Dist.** 1.25 miles By arrangement.

Bollin Hotel, 58 Manchester Road, Altrincham WA14 4PJ (0161) 9282390. £16-19. 5s3t2f **Dist.** 1 mile. Near Altrincham centre (pubs & restaurants)

Old Mill Hotel, 2 Barrington Road, Altrincham WA14 1HH (0161) 9282960. £20-25. 12 rooms, all en-suite **Dist** 1.25 miles

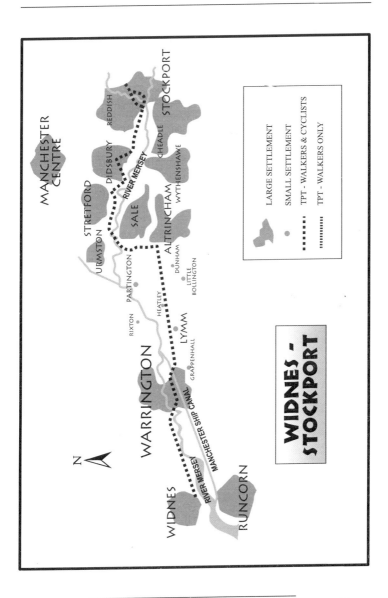

Brooklands Lodge Guest House, 208 Marsland Road, Sale M33 3NE (0161) 9733283. £23.50 ◆◆◆◆ ➷ 1s2d1t1f 🍽 🚲 **Dist.** 1.5 miles. Jacuzzi.

Palatine Hotel, 88 Palatine Road, West Didsbury M20 3JW (0161) 4462222 £22.50 ◆◆◆ ➷ 11s10d5t ♟ **Dist:** 1 mile

Northumbria House, 35 Corbar Road, Stockport SK2 6EP (0161) 4834000. £18-20. ➷ 2 rooms 🍽 ⬚ (by arrangement) ♟ 🚲 **Dist.** 1.5 miles Non-smoking.

HOSTELS & CAMPSITES

Hollybank Caravan Park, Warburton Bridge Road, Rixton, Warrington WA3 6HU (0161) 7752842. ⬚ ♟ 🚲 ✗ **Dist.** 2 miles. Toilets, showers and small shop.

FOOD & DRINK

Ferry Tavern alongside trail on St Helens Canal. Meals Mon-Sat 12-2 & 6-9. Bar snacks / full menu. Boddingtons, Courage, Ruddles. Over 250 whiskies! (01925) 791117

Stockton Heath All the usual high street facilities plus a selection of restaurants and pubs. Just off trail up busy road. Morrisons next to trail at Stockton Heath.

Rams Head, Grappenhall village. Food all day. Sandwiches to a la carte. Boddingtons, Tetley and Pedigree beers. (01925) 262814.

Lymm Excellent range of shops and cafes from fish and chips to upmarket bistros. Supermarket, grocers and plenty of pubs.

Heatley Green Dragon and **Railway** pubs do food. **La Boheme** French restaurant opposite Green Dragon, around £10-15 per head (01925) 753657.

Two pubs in **Dunham Woodhouses**, both doing food.

Dunham Massey Hall Historic house has cafe/restaurant and toilets. 1 mile from route. See attractions below for more details.

Sale Water Park Deckers Restaurant plus small cafe at visitor centre. Toilets. See Attractions overleaf for more details on the water park.

Row of convenience shops on Merseybank Avenue near **Chorlton Water Park**. See Attractions overleaf for more details.

Church Road, Northenden. Just off trail before it passes under M63 (exit at **Tatton Arms** which also does food).Traditional fish & chips. Also take-aways and pubs around the B5167 (Palatine Road) as it passes through Northenden. Pubs and eateries in **Didsbury** centre.

Stockport Cafes and restaurants plus Tuesday, Friday and Saturday markets.

ATTRACTIONS

Widnes-Runcorn Bridge Impressive local landmark.

The Cycle Museum, Mersey Road, High Street, Runcorn. History of the pedal cycle, cycle motors and accessories. Some you can try out. Database of restorers and spares. Telephone (01928) 588524.

St Helens Canal Significant traffic-free trail utilises the towpath of this canal that joins the Manchester Ship Canal with the Mersey estuary. One of Britain's oldest canals. Massive cooling towers of Fiddlers Ferry power station a notable landmark on this section. Good views across the Mersey Estuary on the later sections. **Catalyst** National museum of the chemical industry at the western end of the canal, near **Spike Island** (visitor centre and toilets). Good views from top floor (0151) 4201121.

Manchester Ship Canal Built to link the city's once great textile industry to the sea. It allows sea-going vessels of almost 15,000 tons to sail almost to the city centre. The TPT uses a short section alongside the canal at south Warrington. For details of weekend cruises along the canal in summer ring Mersey Ferries on (0151) 3301444.

Grappenhall Modern commuter suburbs hide quaint old village. Cobbled street, church and two pubs (see Ram's Head entry, pg22).

Lymm Charming village with unusual stocks and market cross on rock outcrop in centre. Attractive rocky gorge runs through village with artificial lake. Bridgwater canal also runs through centre; one of the earliest canals, built by the Duke of Bridgwater to exploit his coal reserves. Country ranger service, information centre (toilets) - on trail.

Dunham Massey Hall Georgian house with superb gardens, 1 mile from the route. National Trust property. Seasonal opening (0161) 9411025.

Sale Water Park Various water sports, from canoes to sailboats and rowboats, on this sizeable lake south of the River Mersey. (0161) 9620118.

Chorlton Water Park Large lakes in former gravel pits. Ideal for anglers, boaters and ornithologists. Toilets (suitable for disabled users). (0161) 8815639.

Wythenshawe Hall, Northenden. Half-timbered 16th century manor house with wide-ranging collection of paintings and furnishings, including Oriental collection. Set in 250 acres of parkland, 1.25 miles from the route. Seasonal opening (0161) 9982331.

Stockport Large industrial suburb that boasts the unusual **Hat Museum** (0161) 3557770. Also **town museum** shows Stockport's history (0161) 4744460. **Art Gallery** has war memorial collection (0161) 4744453. **Floodlit viaduct** dominates much of the town and claims to be Europe's largest brick structure. Underground passages cut into rock underneath the town prior to WWII, and used as war shelters, can now be toured. Tel (0161) 4741940.

Fiddlers Ferry Tavern on the St. Helens Canal, near Warrington (section 2)

INFORMATION FILE

Tourist Information
Warrington: 21 Rylands Street (01925) 632571
Altrincham: 20 Stamford New Road (0161) 9125931
Stockport: Greylaw House, Chestergate (0161) 4744444
Hospitals Altrincham General, Market Street (0161) 9286111. Minor injuries.
More major injuries should go to Wythenshawe.
Wythenshawe Hospital, Southmoor Road (0161) 9987070.
Stepping Hill Hospital, Poplar Grove, Stepping Hill, Stockport (0161) 4831010.
Banks High Street banks in Lymm, Stockton Heath, Altrincham, Sale and
Stockport.
D&M Cycles, 2-4 Hood Lane, Great Sankey, Warrington (01925) 653606
30 yards from the trail. Repair service.
Heatley Cycles directly on the trail heading east out of Lymm (01925) 753424.
Lebrams, 197 Manchester Road, West Timperley, Altrincham (0161) 9286600.
Devereux Cycles, 45 Green Lane, Ashton on Mersey, Sale (0161) 9735234.
A1 Cycle Centre, 414-416 Palatine Road, Northenden (0161) 9982882.
Bardseys Cycles, 482 Manchester Road, Stockport (0161) 4324936. Specialists
in wheel building and repair services but also general sales and repairs.

Market cross and stocks on rock outcrop, Lymm, near Warrington (section 2)

Viaduct carrying disused railway over Manchester Ship Canal, near Grappenhall,
Warrington (section 2)

3 STOCKPORT - PENISTONE

Section Distance 29 miles / 47km

The Route The Apethorn-Godley railpath runs to the south of Hyde, whilst walkers have the option of ascending over the lovely Werneth Low Country Park, with great views over Tameside and the west of the Peak District. A mixture of cycle lane, road, track and footpath options, broadly following the Tame Valley, lead to Hadfield and the railpath known as the Longdendale Trail. On the Longdendale Trail, near Woodhead Tunnel, a short, steep climb leads to rougher bridleway over some fine Dark Peak moorland landscape between Langsett Moors and Longside Moss and on to Salters Brook. After a steep road descent to Dunford Bridge the easy, flat Upper Don Trail leads through rolling, green countryside to the market town of Penistone. All in all, this is a remarkably easy crossing of a significant range of upland moors. Even so, you should be aware that ' the tops' of the Dark Peak area can disappear into thick rolling mist, wind or rain at any time of the year even though the weather in the valley below may be fine and still. More often than not there will be a fresh wind on the moors and the temperature will feel a few degrees cooler than down below. Near Salters Brook you are at the highest point on the whole TPT at 435 metres (1427 feet).

HOTELS & GUESTHOUSES

Old Rectory Hotel, is found in beautiful Haughton Dale, just off the trail next to the pretty Tame Valley. Food and drinks available to non-residents. Call (0161) 3367516 for more details.

Needhams Farm, Uplands Road, Werneth Low, Gee Cross, Hyde SK14 3AQ. (0161) 3684610 Fax (0161) 3679106 📧 charlotte@needhamsfarm.co.uk / www.needhamsfarm.co.uk £16 ◆◆◆ 🛌 1s4d1t1f 🍽 🍽 👕 🚲
Dist. 0.5 miles from walkers' option and 1.25 miles from multi-user route.

There is a **Premier Lodge** at Mottram, near the junction of the M67, A57 and A560, just north of the trail in the Hattersley-Broadbottom area (0870) 7001478. Ring for more details.

Brentwood Guesthouse, 120 Glossop Road, Charlesworth SK13 5HB (01457) 869001. £20 ◆◆◆◆ 🍽 ⦿ 👕 🚲 **Dist.** Near route 🚌

Avondale, 28 Woodhead Road (B6105), Glossop SK13 7RH (01457) 853132. ◆◆◆◆ From £20. 🍽 👕 🚲 **Dist.** 1.25 miles

Kings Clough Head Farm, Off Monks Road, Glossop SK13 6ED (01457) 862668. £18 🛌 1s2d1t 🍽 ⦿ 👕 🚲 **Dist.** 2 miles 🚌

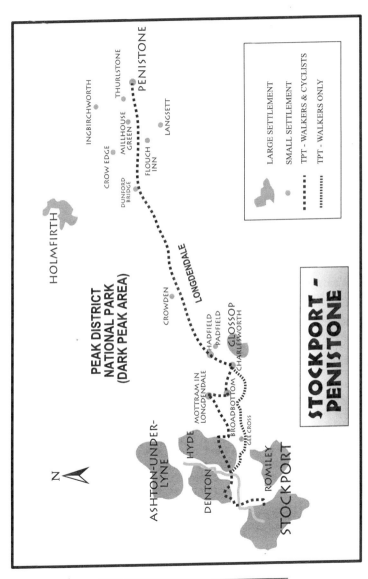

STOCKPORT – PENISTONE

Key:
- LARGE SETTLEMENT
- SMALL SETTLEMENT
- TPT – WALKERS & CYCLISTS
- TPT – WALKERS ONLY

Locations shown: PENISTONE, THURLSTONE, INGBIRCHWORTH, MILLHOUSE GREEN, LANGSETT, CROW EDGE, FLOUCH INN, DUNFORD BRIDGE, LONGDENDALE, HOLMFIRTH, PEAK DISTRICT NATIONAL PARK (DARK PEAK AREA), CROWDEN, GLOSSOP, HADFIELD, PADFIELD, CHARLESWORTH, MOTTRAM IN LONGDENDALE, BROADBOTTOM, GEE CROSS, HYDE, ASHTON-UNDER-LYNE, DENTON, ROMILEY, STOCKPORT

N

Windy Harbour Farm Hotel, Woodhead Road (B6105), Glossop SK13 7QE
(01457) 853107. £22.50 💻 www.peakdistrict-hotel.co.uk 🔌 4s3d1t1f
🍴 🍴 ▪️ 🐕 🚲 **Dist.** 1.5 miles. 🚌 Licensed bar, restaurant and tearoom.

The Gables Hotel, 87 Station Road, Hadfield SK13 1AR (01457) 868250.
💻 welcome@gableshotel.com www.gableshotel.com £22.50♦♦♦ 🔌 6d2t
🍴 🍴 🐕 **Dist.** 0.25 miles.Licensed. Close to Hadfield railway station.

Peels Arms, 6 Temple Street, Padfield SK13 1EX (01457) 852719
£20 🔌 2d2t ♦♦♦🍴 🍴 ▪️ 🐕 🚲 **Dist.** 0.25 miles🚌

Stanhope Arms, Dunford Bridge S36 4TF (01226) 763104
💻 stanhope@zoom.co.uk £22.50 R 🔌2d2t1f singles if required 🍴 🍴 🚲
Dist. Next to the trail.

Carr House, Royd Lane, Millhouse Green, Penistone S36 9NY (01226) 762917.
£12.50B&B, £6 upwards for groups. 🔌Both B&B and bunkhouse accommodation
for groups. 🍴 on request 🍴 🐕 🚲 **Dist.** 1 mile 🚌

Old Crown Inn, Market Street, Penistone S36 6BZ (01226) 7624222. £20 up.
R. 🔌 4s1d1t 🍴 🍴 ▪️ 🐕 🚲 **Dist.** 0.25 miles

Old Vicarage Guest House, Shrewsbury Road, Penistone S36 6AA
(01226) 370607 💻enquiries@old-vicarage.co.uk / www.old-vicarage.co.uk
£25-55. R 🍴 (lunches only in attached teashop) 🍴 ▪️ 🐕 🚲
Dist. Only about 50m off the trail

View over Hyde from walkers' option at Werneth Low Country Park (section 3)

HOSTELS & CAMPSITES

Lymefield Farm Caravan & Camping Site, Broadbottom, Hyde SK14 6AG (01457) 764094. £5 per tent. **Dist.** Just off the route in Broadbottom, down track to Lymefield visitor centre. Same ownership as nearby nursery with tearoom.

Crowden Camping and Caravanning Club Site, Crowden, Hadfield SK14 1HZ (01457) 866057. From £6.90 per night. Open End of March-September. 45 pitches. Hot showers and toilets. 5 miles to shops in Hadfield so stock up on food. **Dist.** 0.75 miles.

Crowden Youth Hostel, Crowden-in-Longdendale, Glossop SK13 1HZ 0870 7705784. £9.50 ⇄ 50 beds - 2 to 6 bedded rooms. 🍽 🍽 ♟ 🚲 Seasonal opening. Self-catering also available. YHA membership required. **Dist.** 0.75 miles. Note nearest village services are 5 miles away in Hadfield.

Langsett Youth Hostel, Langsett, Stocksbridge S36 4GY 0870 7705912. YHA membership required. For group bookings in advance call 0870 2412314 £8.75 ⇄ 27 beds in 4,5 and 6 bed dormitories. ♟ 🚲 **Dist.** 1.25 miles south of trail, along busy, fast A616 . Official YHA hostel with basic facilities. There is a cafe in the Langsett village and **Waggon and Horses** pub serves food.

Also camping at **Windy Harbour Farm Hotel** - call for details - see opposite page. 'Overflow' capacity at **Blackshaw Farm** nearby (01457) 869447. **Dist.** 1.5 miles

Bridleway section above Longdendale Trail (section 3)

FOOD & DRINK

Old Rectory Hotel, set in beautiful Haughton Dale, just off the trail, has food and drinks avaialble to non-residents (0161) 3367516.

Reddish Vale Cafe and toilets at visitor centre. See attractions section below for more details.

Mottram in Longdendale has a reasonable selection of pubs and cafes just off the route.

Lymefield Visitor Centre, Broadbottom Toilets available in visitor centre itself and cafe inside adjacent nursery. Visitor centre (01457) 765780. Entrance opposite **Cheshire Cheese** pub. Also in Broadbottom is the **Harewood Arms** pub and restaurant, with a classy, appetising sounding menu (01457) 763383.

Charlesworth Two pubs en route with the **George and Dragon** serving food. At Gamesley the **Centurion** pub has meals and snacks.

Hadfield main street has a selection of cafes and pubs.

Vale House Farm, Tintwistle. Tel (01457) 869681 for opening details. Tea garden adjacent to Vale House Reservoir. 500m from walking route. Cakes, soups, snacks, teas etc.

Peel Arms Pub in Padfield does food (01457) 852719.

Stanhope Arms, Dunford Bridge (01226) 763104. Lunches and evening meals except Mondays (bar snacks only on Monday). 12-2 & 7-9. 12-8 Sundays.

Penistone has a smattering of cafes, pubs and restaurants.

ATTRACTIONS

Reddish Vale Country Park Local nature reserve and centre of a well developed network of bridleways and tracks (0161) 4775637.

Melandra Roman Fort Scheduled ancient monument near the trail between Gamesley and Hadfield. Accessible on foot from the TPT.

Glossop Appearance as dour cotton town hides pretty 17th century conservation area. All large town services about 1.5 miles off TPT. **Heritage Centre** in town centre (01457) 869176.

Longdendale Valley houses the Longdendale Trail, part of the TPT, and a string of impressive reservoirs. Located in ' Dark Peak' area of Peak National Park just north of the forbidding peaty mass of Bleaklow. Navvies who worked on this former railway line are buried in Woodhead Chapel.

Penistone Pennine market town. 13th century church and 18th century Cloth Hall and Shambles.

Hale's History Tree, carved from a dead beech tree.
Found on Church Road, Hale (section 1)

A sunny summer Sunday means a busy TPT section by the A1 bridge over the River Don (section 4)

The TPT uses the picturesque River Don towpath at Sprotbrough Lock (section 4)

Summer flowers on the TPT near the Earth Centre (section 4)

Riding on the TPT in Greno Wood (section 5)

Bridleway section of TPT above
Longdendale Trail (section 3)

INFORMATION FILE

Tourist Information
Glossop: The Gatehouse, Victoria Street (01457) 855920
Hospitals No major hospitals on this section across the Pennines.
Banks Main high street banks in Glossop. HSBC with cashpoint in Penistone.
Bike Parking 4 enclosed metal bike lockers at Penistone train station (own lock needed).
🚲 **High Peak Cycles** 93-94 High Street, West Glossop (01457) 861535
KG Bikes, 18 Norfolk Street, Glossop (01457) 862427
Lex's Cycles, 112 Sheffield Road, Penistone (01226) 763763

Cyclists at Bullhouse Bridge, Upper Don Trail (section 3)

Cafe in Hadfield, named after the BBC's *League of Gentlemen* comedy (section 3)

4 PENISTONE - BENTLEY

Section Distance 29 miles / 47km

The Route At Oxspring you have a choice of two TPT routes. The main, more direct, option leaves the Upper Don railway path at Oxspring, linking via track, road and footpath to another railway path, the Dove Valley Trail.

Alternatively, you can stay on the railway path at Oxspring, heading south, following the Upper Don and Timberland Trails and the Elsecar Greenway using a variety of surfaces on lanes and bridleways to rejoin the main line of the TPT just east of Wombwell (this option also leads to the Chesterfield Spur - see chapter 5 for details). This alternative passes through the interesting villages of Wortley and Elsecar.

On this section the bleaker foothills of the Pennines around Penistone turn to rolling green countryside. Passing through the regenerated former Wath / Manvers coalfield area your surroundings become increasingly scenic, culminating at the lovely Don Gorge section between Conisbrough and Bentley. Scars on the landscape left by coal mining's decline still remain, but regeneration has gone a long way to making this an attractive countryside area.

HOTELS & GUESTHOUSES

Wortley Hall, Wortley S35 7DB (0114) 2882100 Fax (0114) 2830695
📧 info@wortleyhall.org.uk www.wortleyhall.org.uk★★ £20 and up
⌨ 3s6d14t7f 🍴 🚲18th century listed building in 26 acres of gardens.
Dist. Near route. Restaurant.

Wortley Guesthouse, Park Avenue, Wortley S35 7DB (0114) 2881864 £26.50
⌨ 1s1t2d 🍴 🍸 📱 🚲 **Dist.** Near route.

Wortley Arms Hotel, Halifax Road, Wortley S35 7DB (0114) 2882245 £25
⌨ 1t1d1f 🍴 12-8.30 daily 🍴 🚲 **Dist.** On trail

Wigfield Guest House, 12 Haverlands Lane, Worsbrough Bridge S70 5NQ
(01226) 206363 £16 room only. Full English breakfast £4.⌨ 2d1t1f. Rooms have utility area - fridge, toaster & microwave. 🚲 Area at rear of house for cleaning, washing and repairing cycles and equipment. **Dist.** Next to trail.

Button Mill Inn, Park Road, Worsbrough S70 5LJ (01226) 282639. £25.
⌨ 2s1d3t1f 🍴 🍴 🚲 ✗ **Dist.** within 0.5 miles.

Keel Inn Hotel, Canal Street, Barnsley S71 1LJ (01226) 289813 £15
⌨ 8 rooms 🚲 **Dist.** 2 miles

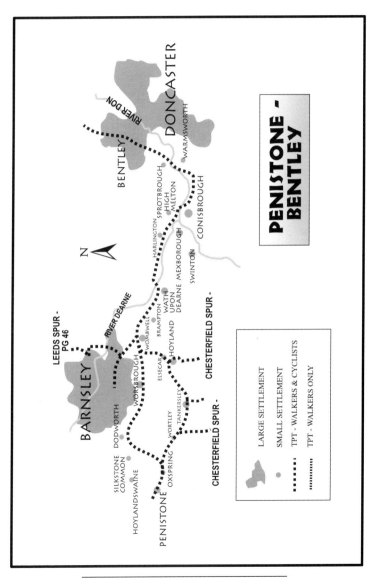

The Earth Centre, Doncaster DN12 4EA (01709) 513933. £20.50 ⟋ 42 rooms including 2 with disabled facilities. All en-suite with TV and hot drinks. 🍽️🍽️ Cycle hire plus try out of alternative style bikes. Accommodation price includes free entry to the Earth Centre itself. **Dist.** On the trail. 🚲 - enquire.
Cosy Terrace Cottage, 4 Trent Terrace, Low Road, Conisbrough DN12 3DN (contact address - 8 Denaby Lane, Old Denaby, Doncaster DN12 4LA) (01709) 580612 / (01709) 585149 £60 per night - whole cottage. ⟋ Sleeps 6-7 people. 🔲 🍽️ 🚲 ✗ **Dist.** 0.25 miles 🚃
Harwoods Guest House, 10 Christ Church Road, Doncaster DN1 2QJ (01302) 342244. From £16 ⟋ 1s2d3t2f 🍽️ 🚲 **Dist.** 1.5 miles
Bay Horse Hotel, Cooke Street, Bentley DN5 0DE (01302) 874414. £19 ⟋ 1s1d2t2f 🚲 **Dist.** 0.5 miles
There is also a **Travel Inn** at **Tankersley** (01226) 350035

HOSTELS & CAMPSITES

Woodland View Caravan Park, 322 Barnsley Road, Hoylandswaine S36 7HA (01226) 761906. £3-4 per unit. Open April-October. **Dist.** 2 miles

Greensprings Touring Park, Rockley Abbey Farm, Rockley Lane, Worsbrough, Barnsley S75 3DS (01226) 288298
💻 www.ukparks.co.uk/greensprings £4.50-7.50 per tent. Open April-October. **Dist.** 2 miles. Cycle hire can be arranged.
The Earth Centre, Doncaster DN12 4EA (01709) 513933. From 2003 there is planned camping provision at £5.00 and bunkhouse accommodation at £10.00. **Dist.** On the trail 🔲 🍽️ Showers and toilets. 🚲 Enquire for secure storage.

FOOD & DRINK

After Penistone opportunites for food and drink thin out considerably.
Waggon & Horses, Oxspring 100 yards from trail. Meals 12-9 Mon-Sat 12-7 Sundays (01226) 763259.
The **Potting Shed Cafe** is on Pot House Lane in Silkstone, 1 mile from the TPT.
Wortley Arms Next to TPT in Wortley village centre. Bar snacks and full meals (0114) 2882245. The **local cafe** is just round the corner.
Harlington Inn, Harlington. Attractive pub, just off the trail, serving food (01709) 892300.
Pastures Lodge, Dearne Bridge, Mexborough. Carvery restaurant (01709) 579599.
Conisbrough Castle Cafe Outside paygate (01709) 863329.
The **Earth Centre** Cafe and toilets (free access). See Attractions for more detail.
Boat Inn Attractive location next to TPT on Don Gorge section approaching Sprotbrough. Choice of bar meals and restaurant. 12-2 & 6-9.30 weekdays. Weekends lunchtime only plus restaurant only on Saturday nights (01302) 857188. There is a cafe at **Cusworth Hall**. See Attractions section for details.
Barnsley town centre (on a 3 mile spur from the main route) and Doncaster town centre (1.5 miles from the main route) have a wide selection of eateries.

Useful information from TPT trail boards in Barnsley (section 4)

Conisbrough viaduct at the western end of the Don Gorge section, Doncaster
(section 4)

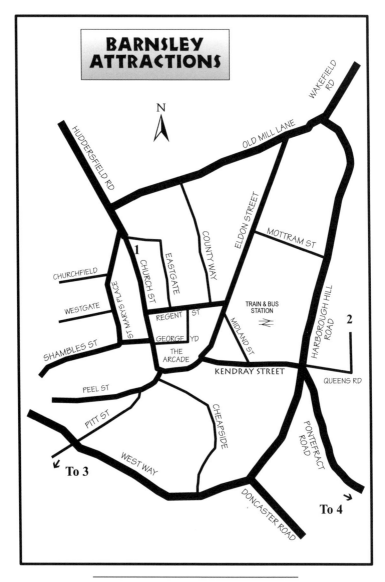

BARNSLEY ATTRACTIONS

N

WAKEFIELD RD

HUDDERSFIELD RD

OLD MILL LANE

ELDON STREET

MOTTRAM ST

1

CHURCHFIELD

CHURCH ST

EASTGATE

COUNTY WAY

ST MARYS PLACE

WESTGATE

TRAIN & BUS STATION

HARBOROUGH HILL ROAD

2

REGENT ST

GEORGE YD

MIDLAND ST

SHAMBLES ST

THE ARCADE

KENDRAY STREET

QUEENS RD

PEEL ST

PITT ST

CHEAPSIDE

PONTEFRACT ROAD

To 3

WEST WAY

To 4

DONCASTER ROAD

ATTRACTIONS

Silkstone Huskar Pit memorial in churchyard commemorating death of 26 children in mining accident. 1 mile north of TPT at western end of Dove Valley Trail.

Worsbrough Mill in Worsbrough Country Park has demonstrations of stoneground flour-making in the water-powered mill. Parts of the building are centuries old. (01226) 774527. **Wigfield Farm** on Haverlands Lane, Worsborough. Ideal family attraction with, shop, cafe and toilets. Admission charge. (01226) 733702. **Rockley Engine House** 17th century blast furnace is nearby.

Barnsley Once a coal mining town that has suffered much due to virtual total pit closure in the area. Local council originated the idea of the Trans Pennine Trail. Large food hall in market (closed Thursdays & Sundays). Attractions (numbered on map) :

1. Cooper Gallery, Church St. Permanent and visiting exhibitions. Cafe. (01226) 242905.

2. Metrodome Leisure Complex, Queens Road. Theme based water rides ideal for kids. (01226) 730060.

3. Locke Park 46 acre park south-west of town centre. Statue of railway builder Joseph Locke and Italianate viewing tower in his wife's memory.

4. Monk Bretton Priory near the start of the Leeds spur, about two miles east of Barnsley town centre. Substantial remains include parts of refectory, gatehouse and 12th century church. English Heritage property - free entry.

Old Moor Wetland Centre Directly on trail near Wombwell. 250 acres of water, marsh and reedbed, ideal for bird watching. Admission charge. Snack bar & toilets. (01226) 751593.

Coal mining was once a huge employer along much of the Dearne Valley but few signs of it remain. The country park, which the TPT runs through before Bolton Upon Dearne, has an interesting feature at its centre which locates former pits in the area and gives a brief industrial history.

Earth Centre, Conisbrough. TPT passes through grounds of this visitor attraction and major lottery project. Admission charge (01709) 513933.

Conisbrough Castle dates from the 12th century and has a spectacular keep. Visible from TPT near Earth Centre. English Heritage - admission charge to non-members (01709) 863329,

Sprotbrough Flash Nature reserve with hides. Mainly waterfowl and riverbank mammals.

Cusworth Hall 0.75 miles from the TPT, featuring Museum of South Yorkshire Life in mansion house plus superb landscaped grounds. Free entry (01302) 782342.

Southern Loop Option Attractions

Wortley Pretty, central square with post office/shop, church, tearooms and pub. **Wortley Top Forge**, Thurgoland. Water-powered iron forge. Open Sundays. (0114) 2817991. **Elsecar** Lovely valley location plus fine conservation area. Once a model village for local colliery workers. **Elsecar Heritage Centre** Directly on the TPT. Former estate workshops housing Newcomen Beam Engine, Bottle Museum and Hot Metal Press. Working steam railway. (01226) 740203. Toilets.

Doncaster City centre 1.25 miles off main route. Despite much modern development the centre boasts some fine older buildings. Numbers refer to map opposite.

1. Mansion House, High Street. The only one outside of York and London. Open only to groups, by appointment. (01302) 734032.

2. St Georges Parish Church, Church Way. Rebuilt by Giles Gilbert Scott in mid-nineteenth century in grand neo-gothic style.

3. Corn Exchange and Market Area Includes wide-ranging food market. Tuesday, Friday, Saturday (01302) 325566.

4. Doncaster Museum & Art Gallery, Chequer Road. Displays on archaeology, natural history, geology, local history and fine art. Adjacent is the Kings Own Yorkshire Light Infantry Museum. Free admission (01302) 734293.

INFORMATION FILE

Tourist Information
Barnsley: Eldon Street (01226) 206757
Doncaster: Central Library, Waterdale (01302) 734309.
Hospitals Barnsley District General, Gawber Road (01226) 730000.
Doncaster Royal Infirmary, Thorne Road (01302) 366666.
Banks All major high street banks in Barnsley and Doncaster town centres.
🚲 **Barnsley Cycle Centre**, 16 Doncaster Road, Barnsley (01226) 287770
Cycosport, 3 Pontefract Road, Barnsley (01226) 204020
Race Scene, 27 Dodworth Road, Barnsley (01226) 215020
Allens Cycles, 23 Barnsley Road, Wombwell (01226) 756281
Factory Direct Bikes, 4 Church Street, Wombwell (01226) 758810
Don Valley Cycles, 10 Chequer Road, Doncaster (01302) 769531
Ride a Bike, Ogden Road, Doncaster (01302) 322239

The attractive Boat Inn next to the trail, near Sprotbrough (section 4)

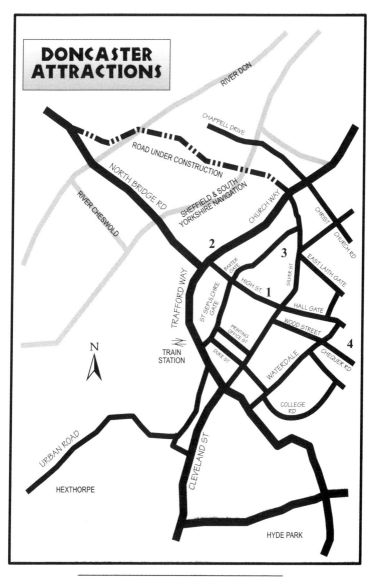

DONCASTER ATTRACTIONS

RIVER DON

CHAPPELL DRIVE

ROAD UNDER CONSTRUCTION

NORTH BRIDGE RD

RIVER CHESWOLD

SHEFFIELD & SOUTH YORKSHIRE NAVIGATION

CHURCH WAY

CHRIST CHURCH RD

2

3

BAXTER GATE

HIGH ST.

SILVER ST

EAST LAITH GATE

1

TRAFFORD WAY

ST SEPULCHRE GATE

HALL GATE

WOOD STREET

4

PRINTING OFFICE ST

CHEQUER RD

N

TRAIN STATION

DUKE ST

WATERDALE

COLLEGE RD

URBAN ROAD

CLEVELAND ST

HEXTHORPE

HYDE PARK

5 BARNSLEY - CHESTERFIELD

Section Distance 35 miles / 55km from Barnsley town centre to Chesterfield town centre using the Wentworth / Beighton option. This is the most complex section in terms of route options, with several route choices heading off the west-east section of the TPT south of Barnsley. There are also spurs to Sheffield and Rotherham centres. Actual distance will, of course, vary depending on your chosen route.

The Route At Oxspring the TPT splits. The southern loop via Wortley, Tankersley and Elsecar rejoins the main line of the TPT just outside Wombwell, but before this you have several opportunities to head off onto the Chesterfield spur. The first comes at Wortley and the second at Tankersley. Both options lead through pretty, rolling green countryside and the large area of woodland north of Grenoside. From here the route picks its way through the suburbs of Chapeltown and Parsons Cross before slotting alongside the River Don at the massive, gleaming Meadowhall shopping complex (a disused railway line is being developed as a more direct alternative along this section). A smaller spur leads off the main route alongside the interesting Five Weirs Walk, towards Sheffield, ending just outside the centre, near the market area. The main route continues south and is nearly all off-road, finally making an impressive entrance to Chesterfield along the lovely Chesterfield Canal.

HOTELS & GUESTHOUSES

Rockingham Arms, 8 Main Street, Wentworth S62 7TL (01226) 742075
From £15.00 (room only) R↴ 12 rooms mainly d&t, some s **Dist.** Very near the most easterly link route from the trail south of Barnsley, down to Sheffield. Breakfast £3.95 continental, full english £5.95. Choice of pub meals 12-9pm.

Middleton Green Farm, Cinder Hill Lane, Grenoside, Sheffield S35 8NH
(0114) 2453279 💻 www.moonmen.co.uk £27.50. R ↴ 3s1d2t1f 🍽 ·
🛏 ⛛ ✗ **Dist.** within 0.25 miles NCN route 6. Sauna & jacuzzi. Near pub.

Travel Inn, Attercliffe Common Road, Sheffield S9 2LU (0114) 2422802
£42.95 for all rooms which can accommodate 2 adults and 2 children. 🍽
⛛ **Dist.** Next to Five Weirs Walk spur into Sheffield city centre.

Swan Hotel, 756 Attercliffe Road, Sheffield S9 3RQ (0114) 2447978
💻 swansheffield@btinternet.com / www.swansheffield.co.uk £24.50 R
↴1s5d2t4f 🍽 ⛛ **Dist.** Near both cyclists' and walkers' spur options about halfway along the spur option into Sheffield city centre.

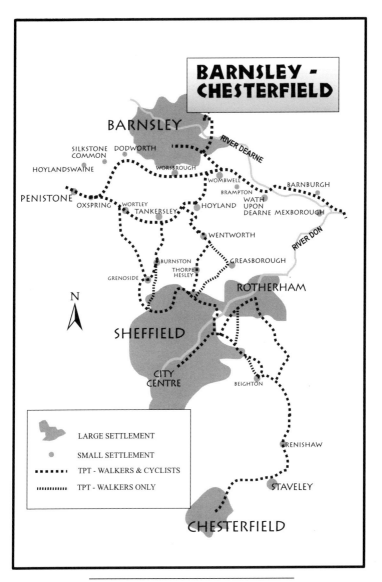

BARNSLEY - CHESTERFIELD

BARNSLEY

RIVER DEARNE

SILKSTONE COMMON
DODWORTH
HOYLANDSWAINE
WORSBROUGH
WOMBWELL
BRAMPTON
BARNBURGH
PENISTONE
OXSPRING
WORTLEY
TANKERSLEY
HOYLAND
WATH UPON DEARNE
MEXBOROUGH
WENTWORTH
RIVER DON
Burnston
GREASBOROUGH
THORPE HESLEY
GRENOSIDE
ROTHERHAM

N

SHEFFIELD

CITY CENTRE
BEIGHTON

Renishaw

STAVELEY

CHESTERFIELD

LARGE SETTLEMENT

● SMALL SETTLEMENT

▪▪▪▪▪▪ TPT - WALKERS & CYCLISTS

▪▪▪▪▪▪ TPT - WALKERS ONLY

The Rutland Arms, 86 Brown Street, Sheffield S1 2BS (0114) 2729003
Fax: (0114) 2731425 ▇www.rutlandarms-sheffield.co.uk £18.50 **R** ｜●｜ (Mon-Fri)
🚲 (outdoor yard) **Dist**. 0.5 miles from TPT Sheffield spur end. 0.25 miles
south of city centre. Bar meals available.

Riverside Court Hotel, 4 Nursery Street, Sheffield S3 8GG (0114) 2731962
£19.50◆◆◆ ▄🏳4s11d8t4f ｜●｜ 🚲 **Dist**. 0.25 miles to the north west of the TPT
end in Sheffield.

Phoenix Hotel, 1 College Road, Rotherham S60 1EY (01709) 364611 £12
upwards (room only - breakfast £5) ◆◆▄🏳 1s2d5t1f ｜●｜
Dist. 0.25 miles. Town centre location, near railway station.

Netherleigh Guesthouse, 97 Gerard Road, Moorgate, Rotherham S60 2PN
(01709) 382753 £12 **R** ▄🏳4s2d5t 🚲 **Dist**. 0.5 miles. Microwave ovens in twin
rooms.

Beighton B&B, 50 High Street, Beighton S20 1EA (0114) 2692004 £16 ◆◆◆
▄🏳 3s1d2t 🚲 **Dist**. 0.25 miles west of trail at northern end of Rother Valley
Country Park.

Foresters Arms, Market Street, Staveley S43 3UT (01246) 477455
▇ www.theforestersarms.co.uk £20 **R** ▄🏳 11 rooms ｜●｜ 🚲
Dist. 0.25 miles. Also a pub with full restaurant menu.

Sitwell Arms, 39 Station Road, Renishaw S21 3WF (01246) 435226 £35
★★★ ▄🏳 29 rooms ｜●｜ **Dist**. Near trail.

Anis Louise Guesthouse, 34 Clarence Rd, Chesterfield S40 1LN
(01246) 235412 ▇neil@anislouise.co.uk / www.anislouise.co.uk◆◆◆ £19.50
▄🏳 1s2d2t **Dist**. 0.5 miles. Near town centre.

Sheffield and Chesterfield have several major luxury hotels and there are quite a
number of B&Bs outside of Chesterfield town centre. Enquire at local information
offices for details. There are several hotels in Rotherham on Moorgate Road,
just to the south of the centre. There are no **hostels or campsites** in the
immediate vicinity of the TPT on this stretch. Those prepared to travel several
miles off the trail can get details of campsites from the relevant tourist information
offices. For example there is one at Thrybergh Park, north-east of Rotherham
and a number several miles south and west of Sheffield.

Chesterfield Canal towpath approaching Tapton Lock (section 5)

FOR ACCOMMODATION SYMBOLS KEY SEE INSIDE COVER

Mock Tudor architecture on Knifesmithgate, Chesterfield (section 5)

FOOD & DRINK

Tankersley Manor Hotel, Tankersley. Food available (01226) 744700. Next to the route just north of Westwood Country Park.

Wentworth has two pubs serving food and an upmarket bistro.

The Acorn, Burn Cross. Lunches and dinners, from meals to bar snacks (0114) 2455009. On the route just to the south-west of Chapeltown.

Plenty of pubs in **Grenoside village**, including **Old Harrow Inn** (snacks and lunches 12-2) (0114) 2399907 and the **Old Red Lion** (food 12-2.30 and 6-8.30, Sundays 12-2.30 only) (0114) 2467383. Village shop / post office.

There are plenty of 'chain' food outlets in the **Meadowhall Shopping Complex**, where the route splits for Sheffield city centre or carries on to Rotherham or Chesterfield.

Wentworth House, on the Five Weirs Walk section into Sheffield, has food and drink (0114) 2441594.

At **Concord Park** the sports centre cafe and golf course club house bar do food and are open to those not using the facilities. See Attractions for details.

Sheffield naturally has plenty of places to eat and drink. One of the more unusual is the **Old Queens Head** on Pond Hill (0114) 2798383. Now a pub it was once a baronial hunting lodge and is the oldest domestic building in Sheffield. Food 11-7 and 12-7 Sundays. The **Fat Cat** and **Kelham Island Brewery** are on Alma Street, north of the centre, near Kelham Island Museum. Real ales and home cooked food. Brewery trips need advance notice (0114) 2494804.

Ulley Country Park, south of Rotherham has toilets and snack machines. (01709) 365332.

In the village of **Ulley** the **Royal Oak** has food lunchtimes and evenings (0114) 2872464

The Mill, on the TPT Chesterfield Canal section 2 miles before Chesterfield, has bar meals and full Sunday lunches (01246) 273807 .

Tapton Lock Visitor Centre, on the Chesterfield canal, has refreshments, information and toilets. Seasonal opening. Phone (01246) 551035 for details.

ATTRACTIONS

Wentworth Attractive village with lots of Victorian architecture located next to the Wentworth estate. 600 feet long frontage of Wentworth Woodhouse stately home (private but walkers' option goes through the grounds).

Thorpe Hesley Once an isolated rural community nicknamed Mutton Town. The Wesley Steps mark the spot where John and Charles Wesley once preached.

Cruck Barn / Concord Park Ranger Station Toilets including disabled facility: ring before visiting to check a ranger is available to arrange access (0114) 2403578. Cafe and toilets approx 150 yards off trail at sports centre and at golf club house (open to public).

Magna UKs first Science Adventure Centre set within vast former Templeborough Steelworks. Have the chance to take control of a JCB digger, feel what it is like to fly or experience the fire tornado. Next to Meadowhall on the Rotherham spur of the TPT (01709) 720002. www.magnatrust.org.uk

For **Sheffield** attractions see pages 44-45.

Rotherham Another South Yorkshire town based on coal and steel industries. Magnificent **15th century parish church** at heart of town. **Chapel of Our Lady** on Rotherham Bridge is one of three bridge chapels in the whole country. The **Clifton Museum** in Clifton Park houses locally made but world-renowned Rockingham porcelain (01709) 823635. **Boston Castle** 18th century folly perched high above the Rother Valley.

Shirebrook Valley Visitor Centre On southern spur out of Sheffield. Within Local Nature Reserve: ponds, meadow, woodland, pleasant picnic spot. Facilities include local history, wildlife displays, bird hide and toilet (suitable for disabled). Open Spring-Autumn, certain days only. Phone (0114) 2735030.

Birley Spa 1800s grade 2 listed Victorian bath house. Just half a mile from the TPT in the Shirebrook Valley. Plunge pool with spring water. Open Sundays April to May. Free entry. (0114) 2735806.

Rother Valley Country Park 750 acres of woods and parkland created from old mineworkings. Bike hire, watersports, golf and fishing available. Visitor centre, toilets (suitable for disabled users) and cafe serving snacks and drinks. Full bar meals available at golf bar near main road entrance (0114) 2471452.

Renishaw Hall and Park Heart of the Sitwell estate with museum, gardens and cafe (01246) 432310. Seasonal opening April-September. Main entrance approx. 1.5 miles from TPT at Renishaw, via A6135 and B6419.

Chesterfield Canal Used for the last stretch of the TPT between Staveley and Chesterfield. Now a pleasant green corridor for walkers and cyclists, it once carried coal and other regional exports from north-east Derbyshire towards the Humber Estuary.

Chesterfield centre is dominated by the bizarrely twisted spire of **St Mary and All Saints Church**, due to unseasoned timber. Monuments to the Foljambe family inside. The **Market Square** is a grand open space with outdoor markets Mondays, Fridays and Saturdays, flea market on Thursdays and farmers' market on 2nd Thursday of the month. The town's **Museum and Art Gallery** has exhibits ranging from Roman coins to the windlass used to construct the famous crooked spire - free admission (01246) 345727. Interesting mock Tudor buildings on Knifesmithgate from 1930s.

Barrow Hill Engine Shed, Campbell Drive, Barrow Hill, Chesterfield (near the trail north of Chesterfield) (01246) 472450 or Chesterfield TIC for details of open days. Preserved railway turntable and workshops.

Revolution House, Old Whittington, Chesterfield (near the trail north of Chesterfield) (01246) 453554. Thatched house, site of a plot against James II. Admission free.

INFORMATION FILE

Tourist Information
Sheffield: 1 Tudor Square (0114) 2211900
Accommodation line (0114) 2011011
www.sheffieldcity.co.uk
Rotherham: Central Library, Walker Place (01709) 835904 www.rotherham.gov.uk
Chesterfield: Low Pavement (01246) 345777 / 8. tourism@chesterfieldbc.gov.uk
Due to move to Rykneld Square end of 2002.
Hospital Northern General Hospital, Herries Road, Sheffield (0114) 2434343
Rotherham District General, Moorgate Road, Rotherham (01709) 820000
Chesterfield & North Derbs Royal, Calow nr Chesterfield (01246) 277271
Banks Several banks in Meadowhall shopping centre, next to route. All major high street banks in Sheffield centre around the junction of Fargate precinct area and High Street. All major banks in Rotherham centre. Staveley has a Lloyds and a Natwest, both with cashpoints. In Chesterfield all major banks with cashpoints are on Market Place and Knifesmithgate.
⍥ **Sheffield Cycle Centre**, 832 Barnsley Road, Sheffield Lane Top, Sheffield (0114) 2570650
O Zone Cycles, 143-147 Fitzwilliam Street, Sheffield (0114) 2752233
Birley Cycle Centre, 52 Birley Moor Road, Frecheville, Sheffield (0114) 2648452
Fosters Cycle Centre, Thames Street, Rotherham (01709) 371756
Sondec Cycles, 222 Wellgate, Rotherham (01709) 369607
JE James, Brimington Rd North, Whittington Moor, Chesterfield (01246) 453453

SHEFFIELD ATTRACTIONS

Known as Steel City and also for knife manufacture and silver plate. WWII bombing destroyed much of the old town and the myriad steel mills have shrunk to a handful. Modern redevelopment has included the introduction of a tram system.

1. Sheffield Anglican Cathedral, Church Street. Architecture from the 15th through to the 20th centuries (0114) 2753434.

2. Cutlers Hall This imposing building houses the Cutlers Company's superb collection of silver. Pre-booked parties only (0114) 2728456.

3. City Museum and Mappin Art Gallery Weston Park. From old masters to Victorian works, plus archaeology and social and natural history. Free admission (0114) 2782600. About 1 mile west of the city centre. www.sheffieldgalleries.org.uk

4. Town Hall Victorian, grade I listed building.

5. Graves Art Gallery Above the city library has an outstanding collection of modern art. Free admission (0114) 2782600 www.sheffieldgalleries.org.uk

6. Kelham Island Museum, Alma Street. Sheffield's industrial past kept alive; including the mighty River Don steam engine (the most powerful in Europe) and a reconstructed Victorian street with actual self-employed cutlers, grinders and hand forgers. (0114) 2722106.

7. Millennium Galleries, Arundel Gate (0114) 2782600. Visual arts exhibitions and Sheffield's Metalwork collection. www.sheffieldgalleries.org.uk

8. Winter Gardens and Peace Gardens Vast new glass construction housing exotic plants next to a newly remodelled central square. See page 78 for more details. To open by end of 2002.

9. Canal Basin Pleasant area in which to sit out and have a coffee.

The Straddle Warehouse, Sheffield and Tinsley Canal Basin, Sheffield (section 5)

FOR ACCOMMODATION SYMBOLS KEY SEE INSIDE COVER

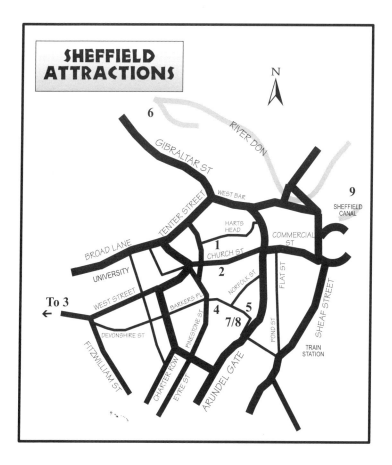

SHEFFIELD ATTRACTIONS

N

6

RIVER DON

GIBRALTAR ST

WEST BAR

TENTER STREET

HARTS HEAD

9

SHEFFIELD CANAL

COMMERCIAL ST

BROAD LANE

1

CHURCH ST

2

UNIVERSITY

NORFOLK ST

FLAT ST

SHEAF STREET

WEST STREET

To 3

BARKERS PL

4

5

7/8

PINESTONE ST

POND ST

DEVONSHIRE ST

TRAIN STATION

FITZWILLIAM ST

CHARTER ROW

EYRE ST

ARUNDEL GATE

Tram outside Cutlers' Hall, Sheffield centre (section 5)

6 BARNSLEY - LEEDS

Section Distance 27 miles / 43 km

The Route Although much of the line of this route might be associated with the collapse of traditional industries, most notably coal mining near Barnsley and Wakefield, it passes through some lovely green spaces. Exiting Barnsley on a railway path, you soon join a fine section along the old Barnsley Canal. Following highlights, linked by resurfaced rights of way and canal towpath, include the charming Heath Common and Heath village then the marina at Stanley Ferry on the Aire and Calder Navigation. The canal is used for your final approach into Leeds, arriving at the Royal Armouries Museum, with a road link for cyclists and separate walking route both ending at City Station.

HOTELS & GUESTHOUSES

Waterton Park Hotel, Walton Hall, Walton, Wakefield WF2 6PW (01924) 257911 £55w/e £62 mid week. ★ ★ ★ ⟲ 11s40d10t ¶● ▪ ❨ ⑧ **Dist.** About 300m off the route, next to the Barnsley Canal. Luxury hotel in Georgian mansion on island. Sauna and golf. Table d'hote evening meal £20.50.

Stoneleigh Hotel, 211 Doncaster Road, Wakefield WF1 5HA (01924) 369461. £27.75-29.75. **R.** ¶● ¶● ▪ ❨ **Dist.** 500m down Doncaster Road towards Wakefield. ⑧ They have a lockable shed for bikes but check this is available when booking.

Bridge Farm Hotel, Wakefield Road, Swillington LS26 8PZ (0113) 2823718. £20-23. ◆◆◆ ⟲ 4s3d3t2f ¶● £10+vat ¶● ▪ ❨ ⑧ **Dist.** 500m

The Comfort Inn, Bishopgate St, Leeds LS1 5DS (0113) 2422555 From £32.50 room only★ ★ ★ ⟲ 5s53d19t3f Breakfast £2.25 continental £4.95 full English **Dist.** 0.25 miles.

Central Hotel, 35-47 New Briggate, Leeds LS2 8JD (0113) 2941456. From £20 ◆◆ ⟲ 8s5d2t11f **Dist.** 0.5 miles.

City Centre Hotel, 51a New Briggate, Leeds LS2 8JD (0113) 2429019. From £25 ◆◆ ⟲ 3s6d6t3f **Dist.** 0.5 miles.

Boundary Hotel Express, 42 Cardigan Rd, Headingley, Leeds LS6 3AG (0113) 2757700. ◼ info@boundaryhotel.co.uk / www.boundaryhotel.co.uk £20-30 **R** ⟲ 6s6d4t2f ¶● ¶● ▪ ⑧ **Dist.** 2.5 miles. By Headingley stadium. Handy if walking / cycling north from Leeds.

There are also a number of luxury hotels in Leeds near the trail end e.g. Queens Hotel, The Marriott. Contact tourist information by the train station for more details. There are no **campsites** in the immediate vicinity of the trail. **Nostell Priory Holiday Park** is 3.5 miles north-east of the Haw Park section and allows camping. (01924) 863938 for more details. The nearest site to Leeds centre is **Roundhay Caravan & Campsite**, 4 miles to the north-east of the centre (0113) 2661850.

FOR ACCOMMODATION SYMBOLS KEY SEE INSIDE COVER

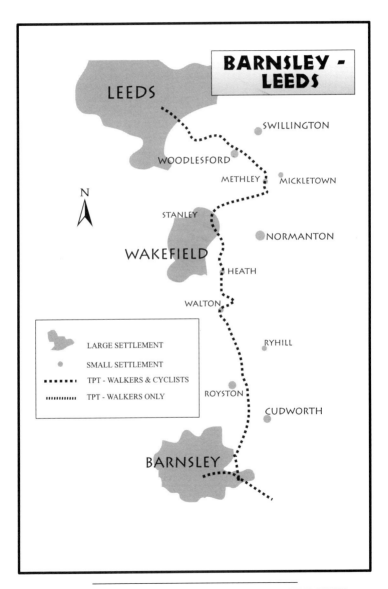

BARNSLEY - LEEDS

LEEDS

SWILLINGTON

WOODLESFORD

METHLEY

MICKLETOWN

N

STANLEY

NORMANTON

WAKEFIELD

HEATH

WALTON

RYHILL

LARGE SETTLEMENT

SMALL SETTLEMENT

TPT - WALKERS & CYCLISTS

TPT - WALKERS ONLY

ROYSTON

CUDWORTH

BARNSLEY

FOOD & DRINK

Squires Tea Room at Waterton Countryside Discovery Centre. Ring (01924) 860282 to check opening hours which vary.

New Inn, Walton. Food available (01924) 255447.

Kings Arms, Heath (01924) 377527. On very scenic section east of Wakefield. Listed building with plenty of nooks, real gas lighting and lovely views over the common. Bar meals and restaurant, lunchtimes & evenings daily (Sunday bar meals available all day). Beer garden. Taylors, Tetleys and Clarks ales.

Plough Inn, Warmfield Lane, Warmfield. About 0.25 miles from the horse riders route. Lunches & dinners (Sunday - lunches only) (01924) 892007.

The Mill House, Stanley, Wakefield. (01924) 290596. Bar / restaurant with family atmosphere. By trail at Stanley Ferry on Aire & Calder Canal. Food lunchtime & evenings, Monday to Friday, all day at weekends.

There are several pubs and fish and chip shops on the road section through **Stanley**.

Rose & Crown, Methley. Food available. (01977) 668235.

Of course, **Leeds** has a huge selection of bars, pubs and restaurants. There is a cafe before the admission till at the **Royal Armouries** (see Leeds attractions, page 50). The Calls area, south-east of the Corn Exchange has more exclusive bars and restaurants, whilst the market has several budget level cafes.

ATTRACTIONS

The Barnsley Canal towpath has been specially renovated for TPT use. Previously the canal, once used to exchange Barnsley coal for supplies from Wakefield, had fallen into neglect. It is now a very pretty section of the route, with reeds and wildlife having colonised much of the waterway. Open countryside alternates with narrow, rocky cuttings.

Waterton Countryside Discovery Centre is at the heart of the Anglers Country Park, an area of woods and lakes east of the Barnsley Canal. Centre 0.75 miles from the route along signed bridleway link. Toilets, cafe, visitor centre and secure cycle parking. For opening details call (01924) 303980.

Walton Hall (see Hotels & Guesthouses section) is the spectacular former home of naturalist Charles Waterton. Many of his strange hybrid taxidermy works and other information are on display at **Wakefield Museum** in the city centre (Wood Street), along with other local history displays (01924) 305356.

Wakefield has its grand **cathedral** at the heart of its pedestrianised shopping centre (01924) 373923 . The **Art Gallery**, Wentworth Terrace, has works by renowned local sculptors Henry Moore and Barbara Hepworth (01924) 305900.

Thwaite Mills, Stourton, Leeds is a former seed crushing and putty mill, now a museum with original water-powered machinery and a steam powered crane. Just off the TPT, on the River Aire, before Knostrop Cut. Admission charge (0113) 2496453.

Look out for **artworks** on the Leeds section of the route.

Family cycling heading along the Aire & Calder towpath into Leeds (section 6)

TPT FOR ALL AGES!

The trail at Charlton Brook near Chapeltown in Sheffield. The TPT utilises many attractive green spaces throughout the city. (section 6)

The eye-catching Millennium Bridge by the trail on your entry into York (section 8)

THE TRANS PENNINE TRAIL - BRIDGING THE GAP

Specially constructed cycle and pedestrian bridge over Ditton Brook (section 1)

Easy, traffic free cycling and plenty of eating and drinking en-route -
Tatton Arms in the Mersey Valley, Greater Manchester (section 2)

TOWN OR COUNTRY? Although the Trans Pennine Trail passes close to many large
cities this isn't often apparent from your surroundings. You could just as easily
be in the middle of the countryside!

Bikers at Knotty Ash, Liverpool - alleged home of Ken Dodd's famous Diddy Men!

New Junction Canal, near Doncaster, South Yorkshire (section 7)

TRANQUILITY ON THE TRANS PENNINE TRAIL
The eastern end of the trail is one of the quietest and flattest areas of the east of England.

Cliffe village, North Yorkshire (cyclists' route) - local village stores provide refreshment stops along the way. Note Millennium milepost (section 9)

Walkers and cyclists along the Aire & Calder canal towpath at Swillington, Leeds
(section 6)

The Kings Arms in an attractive location by the TPT on Heath Common, Wakefield
(section 6)

INFORMATION FILE

Tourist Information
Wakefield: Town Hall, Wood Street (01924) 305000
Leeds: Gateway Yorkshire, The Arcade, City Station (0113) 2425242
Hospitals Pinderfields Hospital, Aberford Road, Wakefield (01924) 201688
Leeds General Infirmary, Great George Street, Leeds (0113) 2432799
Banks Major high street banks in Wakefield centre around Wood Street / precinct
area and in Leeds centre around the Trinity Street shopping area.
捰 **A1 Cycles**, 130 Doncaster Road , Wakefield (01924) 362532
Halfords Superstore, 78 Ings Road, Wakefield (01924) 387474
Psycles Discount Bikes, 174 Kirkgate, Wakefield (01924) 332213
The Bike Chain (inside YHA Adventure Shop), 119-121 Vicar Lane, Leeds
(0113) 2465339. 0.5 miles from route, repair service.

LEEDS ATTRACTIONS

Leeds combines a modern shopping centre with some grand Victorian
architecture. Several attractive shopping arcades in the modern centre. Many
former industrial buildings alongside the River Aire have been renovated for
housing or offices. Numbers refer to map opposite.

1. Dark Arches Bridge lies beneath the vaulted ceiling of the massive railway station
viaduct and has been compared to catacombs. It leads to **Granary Wharf Craft
Arcade**.
2. Calls Footbridge Elegant suspension bridge with a good view down this renovated
area of the River Aire.
3. Thwaite Mills Industrial Museum Alongside TPT before your entry into city centre.
Previously used for a great variety of grinding activities including the production of oil,
dye, corn and putty. Now houses restored water and steam powered machinery (0113)
2496453.
4. Royal Armouries New home of the national arms and armour collection. Five
themed galleries plus demonstrations of jousting, falconry and horsemanship.
Admission free (0113) 2201999 www.armouries.org.uk
5. Victorian Town Hall with giant columns and 225ft clock tower. The **Art Gallery**,
next door, has a strong collection of paintings.
6. Market Hall Beautiful, complex structure of glass, iron and stone with a huge
choice of food.
7. Corn Exchange Unique roof caps this oval building. Now houses speciality shops.
White Cloth Hall behind Corn Exchange undergoing similar restoration.
8. Armley Mills on Canal Road was once the world's largest woollen mill. Now an
industrial museum. Working machinery. Steaming up days for locomotive 'Jack'.
Admission charge (0113) 2637861.

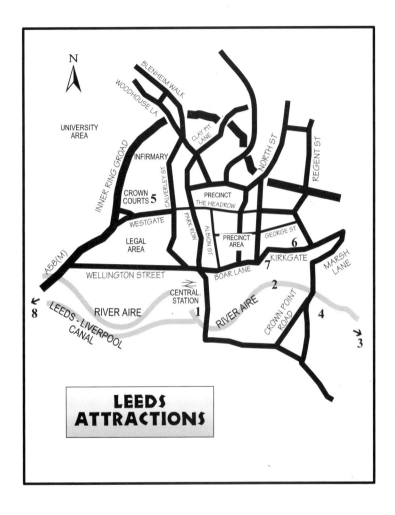

LEEDS
ATTRACTIONS

7 BENTLEY - SELBY

Section Distance 29 miles / 47km

The Route Pleasant red brick villages dot the flat agricultural land of South and North Yorkshire as you shadow the River Don, flowing north towards the Ouse. Agriculture's open expanse is broken by numerous huddles of trees, such as Owston Wood before a quiet road link leads onto the dead straight and very peaceful New Junction Canal. All the while the cooling towers of more easterly power stations loom on the horizon. Minor roads and tracks are then used before you follow the Selby Canal into the market town of Selby, whose highlight is the outstanding medieval abbey. This is a relatively quiet and sparsely settled section of the TPT, so it may well pay off to plan where you are staying and book in advance. Although there is a reasonable amount of accommodation in Selby there are fewer opportunities in the succession of small villages before this. Food and drink opportunities are also limited so try to tie in with opening hours.

HOTELS & GUESTHOUSES

Brian Hall, Fieldgate, Mill Field Road, Fishlake DN7 5GH (01302) 846293 brian@fishlakefinefoods.freeserve.co.uk £25 **Dist.** 2 miles people only. Smallholding with cafe.
Belmont Hotel & Restaurant, Horsefair Green, Thorne DN8 5EE (01405) 812320 www.belmonthotel.com ★★ £40 mid-week £25 weekend 5s10d8t **Dist.** 4 miles For walkers only.
Brewers Arms Hotel, Pontefract Road, Snaith DN14 9JS (01405) 862404 £25 7s3d plus extra annex capacity **Dist.** 0.25 miles.
Forresters Arms, High Street Carlton DN14 9LY (01405) 860315. From £20.50 R. **Dist.** 0.25 miles

Royal Oak Inn, Main Street, Hirst Courtney YO8 8QT (01757) 270633. £25 ♦♦♦ 2s3d5t1f **Dist.** Next to route. Camping also allowed - see camping entry.

Hazeldene, 34 Brook Street, Selby YO8 4AR (01757) 704809. www.hazeldene-selby.co.uk £22-23 ♦♦♦ 2d3t **Dist.** 0.5 miles. Bikeshop nearby. Near town centre services.

Londesborough Arms Hotel, Market Place, Selby YO8 0NS (01757) 707355 From £28.50 **Dist.** 0.25 miles.

The Willows, Cockrett Close, Off White Street, Selby YO8 4BS (01757) 701271 £20 **Dist.** 0.5 miles.

CAMPSITES

Royal Oak Inn, Main Street, Hirst Courtney YO8 8QT (01757) 270633. 24 hour access to toilets. Plenty of pitches. Up to £3 per night. **Dist.** On the route.

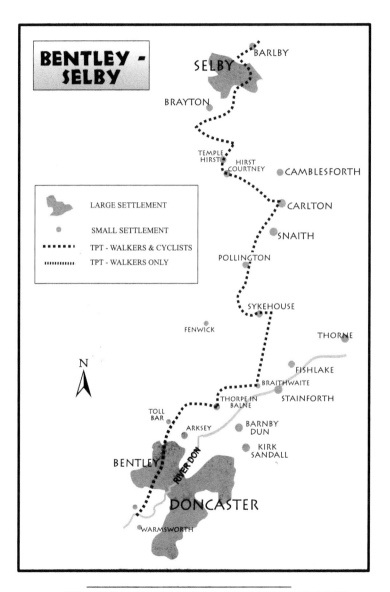

Brian Hall, Fieldgate, Mill Field Road, Fishlake DN7 5GH (01302) 846293
Camping pitches £4.50 per tent Showers, toilet and washing facilities. Cafe.

FOOD & DRINK

Plough Inn, Arksey. Attractive village setting 1.25 miles east of TPT. Food available (01302) 872472.

Brian Hall at Fieldgate just north of **Fishlake** has a cafe on his smallholding. See previous page for details.

Owston Park Lodge, on A19 west of Owston Wood section, 1.25 miles from the route (01302) 700571. Food all day, ranging from sandwiches to chefs specials. Part of Tom Cobleigh chain.

Sykehouse Old George Inn has restaurant. Ring for opening hours (01405) 785635.

Royal Oak Inn at Hirst Courtney does lunches and evening meals (01757) 270633. Plenty of pubs in **Snaith** and lots of eateries in **Selby**, including an Italian bakers at the indoor market.

ATTRACTIONS

Arksey Tiny but delightful village centre with church, almshouses and pub.

Fishlake village was once an inland port. Sign by post office details village history. Green picnic area here was formerly a landing stage for fishermen on the once wide river. Ancient church doorway has extremely rare and fine Norman carving.

Snaith Variety of shops and pubs. Elegant church is the central village landmark.

Carlton Home to Victorian Gothic mansion house, **Carlton Towers**. Once a conventional Jacobean House, it was turned into a mock medieval construction by two young eccentrics in the 1870s. Now a private building that you glimpse from the main road. Occasionally open for weekend events.

Selby Town centre dominated by the superlative **Abbey**, a mix of styles from Norman times onwards. Most impressive feature is the nave, with its rows of Norman arches 'stacked' upon each other. The **Washington Window** is also rightly famous. Next to the Abbey the broad **market place** is joined by Finkle Street, leading to Micklegate, in the heart of the town with some fine old buildings. The old **dock and shipyard** area is lined with impressive edifices along Ousegate.

Looking down New Junction Canal (section 7)

INFORMATION FILE

Tourist Information
Park Street, Selby (01757) 703263
A&E Hospital War Memorial Hospital, Doncaster Road, Selby (01757) 702664.
Banks HSBC in Snaith, no cashpoint. Lloyds, Barclays, HSBC, Natwest and Halifax (Link) all with cashpoints around Market Place, in front of the Selby Abbey.
 **Forward Cycle Store**, 87 High Street, Bentley (01302) 874164
Robson Cycles, 78 Owston Road, Carcroft (01302) 722275. 2.25 miles west of the route at Owston Wood. **JT Donoghue**, 8 The Crescent, Selby (01757) 706037 **Selby Bike Centre**, 49 Gowthorpe, Selby (01757) 702385

Selby Abbey (section 7)

8 SELBY - YORK

Section Distance 18 miles / 29 km

The Route Flat agricultural land once again makes for easy going. There are a number of small, attractive red-brick villages near the route before the final passage of the TPT through Bishopthorpe and into the outskirts of York. The final approach to the historic core of York is a fine one, passing over the racecourse and alongside the River Ouse at Rowntree Park. After passing along the river and through the centre you finish at the grand train station. Much of the section is on the excellently surfaced York - Selby Railpath, with path and road links at either end.

HOTELS & GUESTHOUSES

Dairyman's Cottage, 14 Kellfield Road, Riccall YO19 6PG (01757) 248532
£22.50 1s1d1t1f (by arrangement) **Dist.** 0.25 miles

South Newlands Farm, Selby Road, Riccall YO19 6QR (01757) 248203
£18-22 ♦♦♦ 2d1t1f Basic tools. **Dist.** 0.25 miles

Avondale Guesthouse, 61 Bishopthorpe Road, York YO23 1NX (01904) 633989.
 www.avondalehouse.co.uk £24 ♦♦♦ **Dist.** 0.25 miles west of the trail at Rowntree Park.

Bowen House, 4 Gladstone Street, Huntington Rd, York YO31 8RF
Tel (01904) 636881. £24 ♦♦♦ 5s/d/t/f **Dist.** 1 mile. Quiet location north-east of the centre, near the River Foss. Ownership changing - double check details when booking.

Mont-Clare Guest House, 32 Claremont Terrace, Gillygate, York YO31 7EJ
(01904) 627054. www.mont-clare.co.uk £30 ♦♦♦ **Dist.** 0.5 miles. Just north of historic minster area.

Riverside Walk, 8-9 Earlsborough Terrace, Marygate, York YO30 7BQ
(01904) 620769 www.bedandbreakfast.co.uk £20-27.50♦♦♦ 2s9d1t
  Dist. 0.25 miles. North of River Ouse, opposite train station.

Romley House, 2 Millfield Road, York YO23 1NQ (01904) 652822
 www.romleyhouse.co.uk £20 ♦♦♦ **Dist.** 0.25 miles

Saxon House Hotel, 71-73 Fulford Road, York YO10 4BD (01904) 622106
Fax (01904) 633764   www.saxonhousehotel.co.uk £25-30 ♦♦♦
Dist. 0.5 miles, on A19, south east of city centre. Residents' bar.

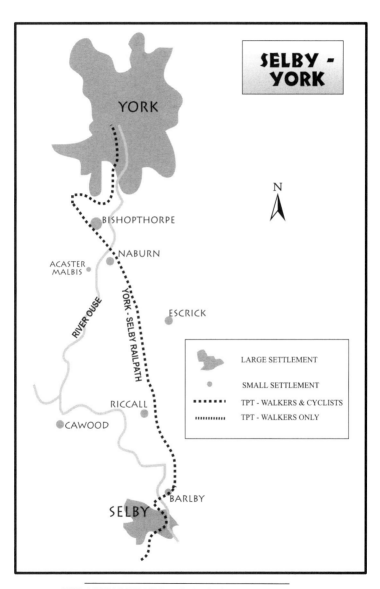

SELBY - YORK

YORK

N

BISHOPTHORPE

NABURN

ACASTER MALBIS

RIVER OUSE

YORK - SELBY RAILPATH

ESCRICK

RICCALL

CAWOOD

BARLBY

SELBY

LARGE SETTLEMENT

SMALL SETTLEMENT

•••••••• TPT - WALKERS & CYCLISTS

••••••••• TPT - WALKERS ONLY

HOSTELS & CAMPSITES

York International Youth Hostel, Water End, Clifton, York YO30 6LP
0870 7706102 ▣ york@yha.org.uk / www.yha.org.uk £16
⟿ Dormitories & s/t/tr ▣ ▣ ▣ ▮ ⚲ Also self-catering, games room, cyber cafe, book exchange and bird watching. **Dist.** 1.25 miles to north of centre.

York Backpackers Hostel, Micklegate House, 88-90 Micklegate, York YO1 6JX
(01904) 627720 ▣ www.yorkbackpackers.co.uk Dormitory £11-12 Double £15. **R.**
⟿ 135 beds. ▣ ▣ ▣ ▮ ⚲ ✗ **Dist.** 0.25 miles. Near centre.
Self-catering facilities, bar & continental cafe, internet access.

York Youth Hotel, 11/13 Bishophill Senior, York YO1 6EF (01904) 625904
▣ www.yorkyouthhotel.demon.co.uk From £10 room only ⟿ 120 beds
▣ ▣ ▮ ⚲ ✗ Self-catering facilities, games room. **Dist.** 0.25 miles 🚌

Naburn Lock Caravan & Camping Park, Naburn YO19 4RU (01904) 728697
14 tent pitches from £9 March - November. Shop, laundry and showers.
▣ nablock@easynet.co.uk **Dist.** 1 mile.

Chestnut Farm Holiday Park, Acaster Malbis YO23 2UQ (01904) 704676
★★★★★ 25 tent pitches from £9. April - October. Wide-ranging facilities including shop, laundry, driers and showers. ▣ www.chestnutfarmholidaypark.co.uk **Dist.** approx. 1.5 miles.

Riverside Caravan and Camping Site, Ferry Lane, Bishopthorpe YO2 1SB
(01904) 704442. 25 units - phone for details **Dist.** 0.5 miles.

Rowntree Park Caravan Club Site, Terry Avenue, York YO2 1JQ(01904) 658997.
Showers, toilets ▣ ▮ 6 tent pitches **Dist.** Nearby trail on your entry to York by the River Ouse. Facilities for disabled.

FOOD & DRINK

Riccall Food outlets and pubs.
Naburn Food at the **Blacksmith's Arms** (01904) 623464.
Bishopthorpe Several village pubs.
Tesco supermarket cafe Handily open 24 hours. Just off trail on Tadcaster Road near college buildings on York outskirts.

York itself has a huge range of eating and drinking places, including some fine historic pubs.

Crossing the Ouse south of Bishopthorpe, near York (section 8)

ATTRACTIONS

Riccall Quiet and pretty village. Norway's Harold Hardrada stopped here in 1066 on his way to defeat by King Harold at Stamford Bridge.
Naburn Lavish Ouse Navigation Trustees banqueting house just south of village cost £3,000 in 19th century!
Bishopthorpe Grand **Bishop's Palace**. Main buildings date from 15th century and chapel from 13th century.

INFORMATION FILE

Tourist Information De Grey Rooms, Exhibition Sq. (01904) 621756.
   ▣ www.york-tourism.co.uk There is also a tourist office at the railway concourse (01904) 621756
Hospital York District Hospital, Wigginton Road (01904) 631313.
 Banks All major high street banks in York Centre.
   ⬥ **Bob Trotter Cycles**, 13-15 Lord Mayors Walk (01904) 622868
Bike Shack, 58 Walmgate (01904) 622044 **Cycle Heaven** 2 Bishopthorpe Road (01904) 636578 **York Cycleworks**, 14-16 Lawrence Street (01904) 626664

YORK ATTRACTIONS

York is so crammed full of historical buildings, pubs, interesting streets and byways and museums that it is impossible to do more than cover the highlights. For a comprehensive guide to historical walks and other city features see 'York Walks' by the same author, from Excellent Books.

• **York Minster** (1) The largest Gothic church in northern Europe, built over a 250 year timespan. The Lady Chapel contains the Great East Window, the size of a tennis court and the largest area of medieval glass in the world. Norman Doomstone and William of York's tomb in crypt. From choir screen look up 200 feet into the massive central tower. Undercroft has Roman remains and you can walk round the massive supports of the central tower. Open daily, except Sunday morning (services only) (01904) 557226.
• The **Treasurer's House** (2) Originally the house of the keeper of the Minster's affairs, it was restored by a 20th century industrialist. April - Oct. Admission charge (01904) 624247. (NT members free). Free entry to tea room / art gallery.
• **Yorkshire Museum** (3) One of the finest collections of archaeology, geology and natural history in the north of England. Open daily (01904) 551800.
• **National Railway Museum** (4) Housed in the old Leeman Road steam depot and a newer building, it includes classics such as Victorian and Edwardian royal carriages and the Mallard. Open daily. (01904) 621261. Free entry.
• **Micklegate Bar** (5) Historically, the most important gateway into the city and famous as the place traitors' heads were exhibited on poles. Houses **Micklegate Bar Museum** telling the story of the **City Walls**. Admission charge.
• **The Shambles** (6) One of the best preserved medieval streets in Europe. Margaret of Clitherow lived at no.39 which is now a shrine to her memory; she was pressed to death with heavy stones for harbouring Jesuits.
• **Merchant Adventurers' Hall** (7) Huge timber-framed building deriving its name from the powerful medieval trading organisation (01904) 654818.
• **Jorvik Viking City** (8) Recreation of a tenth century Coppergate Alley. Perhaps the strongest reminder of the Vikings' presence in the city is the 'gate' ending of many street names. Open daily. Admission charge (01904) 543403.
• **Clifford's Tower** (9) The original wooden Norman fortress here was later replaced with stone and was once used as the Royal Mint. Its name comes from Roger Clifford, hung from the tower wrapped in chains in the 14th century. Magnificent views from the upper rim. Open daily. Admission charge (01904) 646940.
• **Castle Museum** (10) England's most popular museum of everyday life. Great visual appeal includes completely reconstructed Jacobean, Georgian, Victorian and 20th century rooms and completely reconstructed Edwardian Street. Open daily (01904) 653611.
• **Barley Hall** (11) Reconstructed townhouse of a medieval York citizen. March-Oct. Admission charge (01904) 610275.

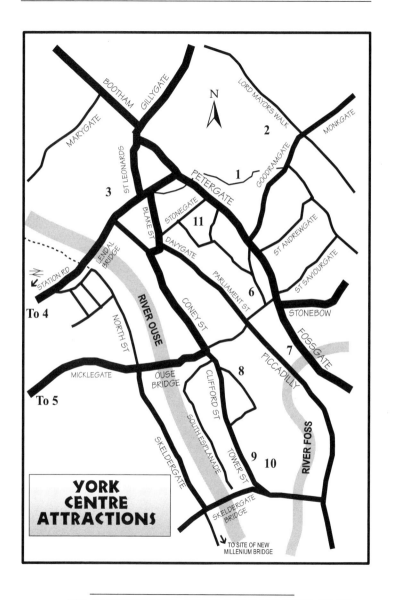

9 SELBY - BROUGH / WELTON

Section Distance   20 miles / 32km

The Route One of the quietest sections on the whole TPT, you follow the slow, wide Ouse through some tiny villages to the base of the Wolds. Population is sparse and Howden, with its highly unusual church, is the only town of any size. Village services become more frequent and wide-ranging as you reach such pretty settlements as Brantingham and Welton at the southern tip of the Yorkshire Wolds. Walkers' and cyclists' routes diverge for considerable distances, walkers more often following the River Ouse's banks. The going is flat, with wide vistas over the river and huge fields.

HOTELS & GUESTHOUSES

Hagthorpe House, Selby Road, Brackenholme near Hemingborough YO8 6EL (01757) 638867 ▉hagthorpe@supanet.com £17-22 ⬒ 1d1t ▣ ▪ ❚
⚅ ✗ **Dist.** On A63 2.25 miles east of the trail through Hemingborough ⛟

Minster View Hotel, 2-3 Corn Market Hill, Howden DN14 7BU (01430) 430447. £18.50 ⬒ 2s5d1t1f ▣ ▣ on request ❚ ⚅ **Dist.** 0.25 miles

Briarcroft Hotel, Clifton Gardens, Goole DN14 6AR (01405) 763024 £24. **R.** ⬒ 5s12d ▣ ❚ ⚅ **Dist.** 2.5 miles from walking route, 3.5 miles from cycling route.

Clifton Hotel, 155 Boothferry Road, Goole DN14 6AL (01405) 761336 ▉ cliftonhotel@telinco.co.uk £24.50 Mon-Thurs £22 weekends ★ ★ ⬒ 4s3d1f ▣ ▣ ▪ ⚅ **Dist.** 2.5 miles from walking route, 3.5 miles from cycling route

Fairways Farm, Northfield Close, South Cave HU15 2EW (01430) 421285. £20. ❚ ⚅ **Dist.** Approx 1.5 miles from cycling route, 2.5 miles from walking route.

Turks Trod House, 67a Church Street, South Cave HU15 2EP (01430) 423931. £20 ⬒ 1d2t ▣ ▪ ❚ ⚅ Basic tools. **Dist.** Approx 1.5 miles from cycling route, 2.5 miles from walking route.

Littleover Lodge Guest House, Hill Top, Howden Croft Hill, Ellerker HU15 2DE (01430) 421821. £16 ◆ ◆ ◆ ▣ ▪ ❚ ⚅ **Dist.** Approx 1.5 miles from cycling route, 2.5 miles from walking route.

Hall Farm, Brantingham, HU15 1QG (01482) 667242 £16 ⬒ 5d ▣ ▪ ❚ ⚅ **Dist.** On route. Quiet location, pleasant gardens.

Rudstone Walk, South Cave (B1230) HU15 2AH (01430) 422230 ▉ rudstone-walk.co.uk £29.50 ⬒ 14 rooms ▣ ▪ ❚ ⚅ **Dist.** 3 miles Self-catering also available ⛟

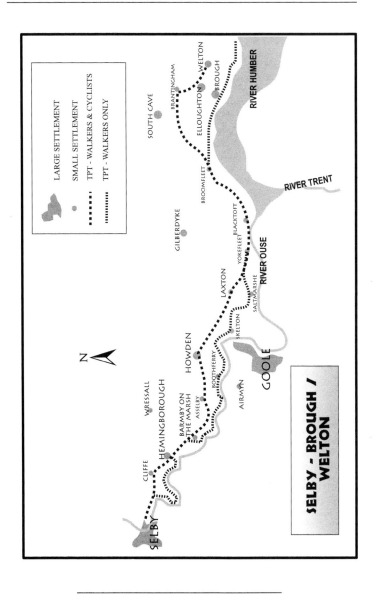

SELBY - BROUGH / WELTON

LARGE SETTLEMENT

SMALL SETTLEMENT

TPT - WALKERS & CYCLISTS

TPT - WALKERS ONLY

N

RIVER HUMBER

RIVER TRENT

RIVER OUSE

WELTON
BROUGH
ELLOUGHTON
BRANTINGHAM
SOUTH CAVE
BROOMFLEET
BLACKTOFT
YOKEFLEET
GILBERDYKE
LAXTON
SALTMARSHE
SKELTON
GOOLE
HOWDEN
BOOTHFERRY
ASSELBY
AIRMYN
BARMBY ON THE MARSH
HEMINGBOROUGH
WRESSALL
CLIFFE
SELBY

Woldway, 10 Elloughton Rd, Brough HU15 1AE (01482) 667666. £16 ♦ ♦♦
🛏1s1d1t 🔲 ⦂ 🍴 🚲 **Dist.** 0.75 miles from walking route, 0.5 miles from
cycling route.
Green Dragon Hotel, Welton has accommodation - see below.

HOSTELS & CAMPSITES

Hope & Anchor Inn, Blacktoft DN14 7YW (01430) 440441. 4 tent pitches. Hot
water, toilets. Pub food available, Weds - Sun, lunchtime & evenings. Next to
route.

FOOD & DRINK

Nearly every small village along the route seems to have its own pub:

Laxton **Bricklayers Arms** serves Sunday lunch and evening meals on selected
days only. Call in advance to confirm food required (01430) 430111. The **Village
Store** in Laxton also serves tea, coffee, scones and teacakes. Open Thurs-
Sun inclusive.
Broomfleet **Red Lion** serves drinks only (01430) 422426.
Blacktoft **Hope & Anchor** (01430) 440441. Campsite as above.
Ellerker has a shop and pub and the a la carte **Black Horse Restaurant** where
3 courses are around £25 (01430) 423270.
Brantingham **Triton** restaurant (01482) 667261.
Elloughton **Half Moon** (01482) 667362.
Welton's **Green Dragon Hotel** Food. Accommodation also. Dick Turpin,
infamous highwayman, captured here in 1739 (01482) 666700.

Time out at Brantingham post office (section 9)

FOR ACCOMMODATION SYMBOLS KEY SEE INSIDE COVER

Weighton Lock where Market Weighton Canal meets the River Humber (section 9)

ATTRACTIONS

190 foot tower of St Marys Church at **Hemingborough**. Pencil-like spire of fine white stone is a landmark for miles around. Inside are fine bench-end carvings. Key from Church House or garage. The main street contains a number of fine 19th century houses.

Howden Small market town dominated by the **Church of St Peter**. The arch of the collapsed 17th century choir remains and dramatically frames the rest of the church. Remains of the ruined chapter house have fine carving. Former **Bishop's Palace** now a private residence but a path to playing fields leads right by it. It was once a stopping place for the medieval Prince Bishops of Durham who controlled vast areas of the locality. Attractive **Market Place** and brick **Market Hall**.

Blacktoft Jetty is important for ships travelling up the Ouse to Goole; it's a handy laying up point to wait at until the tide has risen enough for them to go on. Ships from all countries dock here, especially from the Baltic area.

Brantingham is perhaps the quaintest of all the villages on this section, with its brick terraces decorated with wooden porches. The village pond is backed by estate land. The elaborate war memorial was built from parts of the old Victorian Town Hall in Hull.

Welton Much grand architecture, for example Welton Grange, created by wealthy Hull shipping merchants who treated the village as a country retreat. Church has Pre-Raphaelite windows made by William Morris's craftsmen.

INFORMATION FILE

ڶ **Discount Cycling**, 115 Pasture Road, Goole (01405) 764045
Banks HSBC banks in Howden and South Cave (1 mile from cycling route), both with external cashpoints.

The Bricklayers Arms at Laxton (section 9)

Stained glass window, village hall, Blacktoft (section 9)

The quiet roads on the cyclists' option, north of the River Humber (section 9)

10 BROUGH / WELTON - HORNSEA

Section Distance 28 miles / 46 km

The Route The interim cycling option continues through the Wolds whilst the walking route maintains its course along the Humber, passing under the truly spectacular Humber Bridge. Through the grand old port of Hull you head onto the Hornsea Rail Trail, which leads through quiet agricultural countryside to the resort of Hornsea, with its traditional seaside food and entertainments. Accommodation planning may be different for walkers, cyclists and horse riders, as the various user route options are separated by up to 2 miles in some places.

HOTELS AND GUESTHOUSES

B&B@103, 103 Ferriby High Road, North Ferriby HU14 3LA (01482) 633637 / mobile 07808 387651 ■ simpson.103@usa.net / www.bnb103.co.uk £15 ♦♦♦ ⌁ 1d1s1t ⑥ **Dist.** approx 1 mile. 🚗

Country Park Lodge, Cliff Road, Hessle Foreshore, Hessle HU13 0HB (01482) 640526. £24.50 ⌁ 8 rooms 🍴 at adjacent Bridge Suite Restaurant. Bar meals also. **Dist.** On walking route, 1.25 miles from cycling route.

Redcliffe House Luxury B&B, Redcliffe Road, Hessle HU13 0HA (01482) 648655. £25 ♦♦♦♦ ⌁ 1s1d2t1f 🍴 ⑥ **Dist.** On walking route. Fridge and microwave.

Acorn Guest House, 719 Beverley High Road, Hull HU6 7JN (01482) 853248. £19 ♦♦♦ ⌁ 9 rooms 🍴 🍽 ⑥ ✗ **Dist.** 1.5 miles.

Admiral Hotel, 234 The Boulevard, Hull HU3 3ED Tel & Fax (01482) 329664. £12.50 ♦♦ ⌁ 2s1t1f 🍴 🍽 ⑥ ✗ **Dist.** Within 0.5 miles of both walking and cycling routes, just over a mile west of Hull centre.

The Arches, 38 Saner Street, Hull HU3 2TR (01482) 211558. £15 ♦♦♦ ⌁ 4 rooms ⑥ **Dist.** Within 0.5 miles of both walking and cycling routes, just over a mile west of Hull centre.

Conway-Roseberry Hotel, 86 Marlborough Avenue, Hull HU5 3JT (01482) 445256 / 07909 517328. £17 ♦♦♦♦ ⌁ 2s2d2t 🍴 ⑥ **Dist.** 1 mile from cycling route, 2.25 miles from walking route.

Earlsmere Hotel, 76-78 Sunnybank, Hull HU3 1LQ (01482) 341977. ■ www.earlsmerehotel.karoo.net £17.50. ♦♦♦ ⌁ 9 rooms 🍴 ⑥ ✗ **Dist.** 0.5 miles from cycling route, 1.75 miles from walking route. Just to the north of West Park, west of Hull centre.

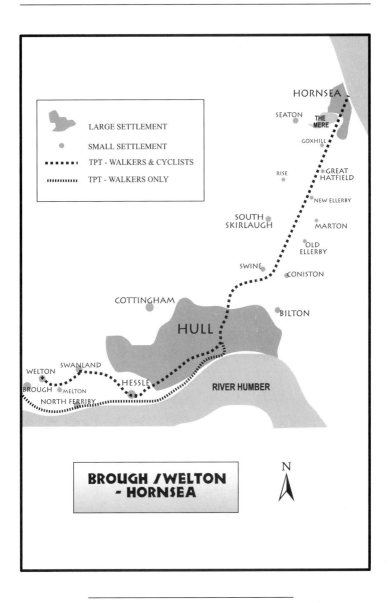

LARGE SETTLEMENT

SMALL SETTLEMENT

TPT - WALKERS & CYCLISTS

TPT - WALKERS ONLY

HORNSEA

SEATON

THE
MERE

GOXHILL

RISE

GREAT
HATFIELD

NEW ELLERBY

SOUTH
SKIRLAUGH

MARTON

OLD
ELLERBY

SWINE

CONISTON

COTTINGHAM

BILTON

HULL

WELTON

SWANLAND

HESSLE

BROUGH

MELTON

NORTH FERRIBY

RIVER HUMBER

**BROUGH /WELTON
- HORNSEA**

N

Quality Royal Hotel, 170 Ferensway, Hull HU1 3UF (01482) 325087.
£42.50. ★ ★ ★ ⟲ 155 rooms ⦿ ⦿ · ⛏ ⮾
Dist. Within 0.25 miles. Fully equipped leisure centre.

Trees Guesthouse, 132 Sunnybank, Hull HU3 1LE (01482) 448822. £16-18.
⟲ 3s2d2t ⦿ ⦿ · ⛏ ⮾ **Dist.** 0.5 miles from cycling route, 1.75 miles
from walking route.

Spaceyfield Bungalow, Thirtleby HU11 4LL (01482) 817713. £15. ⦿ ⦿
· ⛏ ⮾ **Dist.** 2 miles. Leave trail at junction with A165, south through
Coniston and turn left. Bungalow well-signed. Smallholding with livestock and
home-produced food. Self-catering also available.

Admiralty Guesthouse & Tearoom, 7 Marine Drive, Hornsea HU18 1NJ
(01964) 536414. £15 R ⟲ 6s7d ⦿ ⦿ ⮾ **Dist.** 100 yds from end.

Ashburnam Guest House, 1 Victoria Avenue, Hornsea HU18 1NH
(01964) 535118. £15. R ⟲ 1s3d1t2f ⮾ **Dist.** 0.25 miles from route end.

Merlstead Hotel, 59 Eastgate, Hornsea HU18 1NB (01964) 533068. £22.50
♦♦♦ ⟲ 1s1d3t1f ⦿ ⮾ **Dist.** 0.25 miles.

Sandhurst Guesthouse, 3 Victoria Avenue, Hornsea HU18 1NH
(01964) 534653 ▣ rhodes@hornsea15.fsnet.co.uk £12-15. R ⟲ 2t1f
⦿ ⮾ **Dist.** 0.25 miles from route end.

Westgate Mews, Back Westgate, Hornsea HU18 1BP (01964) 533430
▣ walker@hornsea14.freeserve.com 1 cottage, 1 flat available - let weekly
but may have daily and shorter lets if available. R · ⛏ ⮾ Self-catering.
Dist. 0.75 miles. Near Hornsea Mere. Cottage sleeps 6. Flat sleeps 4.

HOSTELS & CAMPSITES

Hull International Hostel, 4 Malm Street, Boulevard, Hull HU3 2TF (01482) 216409
£10 shared room £12 single - room only- light breakfast £1 · **Dist.** Within 0.5
miles of both walking and cycling routes, just over a mile west of Hull centre.
Self-catering facilities available.
Burton Constable Caravan & Camping Park, Old Lodge, Sproatley HU11
4LN (01964) 562508. ★ ★ ★ ★ Toilets plus showers. ⛏ ⮾ **Dist.** Approx. 3
miles east of Hornsea Rail Trail, in the lovely grounds of Burton Constable Hall.
Spaceyfield Bungalow, Thirtleby HU11 4LL (01482) 817713. £4 per pitch.
See above for details of B&B accommodation. Self-catering also available.

Cowden Caravan & Leisure Park, Eelmere Lane, Cowden HU11 4UL (01964) 527393 **R.** 🔲 ✗ **Dist.** 3.5 miles south of Hornsea. March1st - Jan 1st. Shop. No camping in 2002 but available again from March 2003.

FOOD & DRINK

Swan & Cygnet, Swanland, serves food (01482) 634571.
Riverside Bar is on the foreshore (walkers' route) at Hessle. A la carte meals and bar snacks. Part of Country Park Lodge accommodation (01482) 640526.
Marquis of Granby Pub, Hessle (on cycling route) (01482) 626251.
The **Railway** public house, nearby the trail at New Ellerby has food (01964) 563770.
If visiting **Burton Constable Hall**, 2.5 miles off the trail, there is a **tea room** just outside the paygate. See Attractions below for more details.
The **Wrygarth** pub at Great Hatfield, next to trail (01964) 536994.
Food and drink is readily available in Hornsea including the chance for traditional fish and chips at **John Sullivan** near the front. Cafe at **Hornsea Mere** (see below).

ATTRACTIONS

Swanland Pretty wolds village with shop and duck pond (cycling route).
The incredible **Humber Bridge** soars above **Hessle**. Walking route passes underneath the bridge but cyclists currently have to make a detour. 533 feet high twin towers and 1542 yard main span hung between them from immensely thick cables. National Cycle Network route number one from Harwich to Hull uses what must be one of the most spectacular cycle lanes in the country, over the bridge. **Humber Bridge Country Park** provides a good viewing place for the bridge alongside woodland walks and the disused windmill of **Cliff Mill**, a former 'whiting mill' used for crushing chalk to be used in paints and putty. The village of Hessle itself, despite being almost swallowed by Hull's suburbs, retains a well-kept village green.
Burton Constable Hall Grand Elizabethan House, 2.5 miles off the Hornsea Rail Trail. 200 acres of Capability Brown parkland. Admission charge. Seasonal opening. (01964) 562400 for details.
Hornsea Sandy beach fronts promenade with traditional seaside attractions. Town centre has attractive buildings and local services. **Hornsea Folk Museum** on main street. Open in summer (01964) 533443.
Hornsea Mere is Yorkshire's largest freshwater lake. Bird reserve plus boating, fishing and **cafe** (01964) 533277.

INFORMATION FILE

Tourist Information
Humber Bridge, Humber Bridge Country Park (01482) 640852
Hull 1 Paragon St (just off Victoria Sq) (01482) 223559. There is also an office at King George Dock (01482) 702118
Hornsea 120 Newbegin (01964) 536404. Seasonal opening.
Hospital Hull Royal Infirmary, Anlaby Road (01482) 328541
Banks All major banks with cashpoints are on or around Whitefriargate precinct area and Victoria Square in Hull. Newbegin (main street), Hornsea has Halifax with Link machine and Natwest with cashpoint. Also HSBC and Lloyds.
🚲 **Steering Wheel Cycle Centre**, 1101-1107 Hessle High Road, Hessle (01482) 352030. **Freetown**, 70-80 Prospect St (01482) 589066. **Bobs Bikes**, 23 Princes Avenue, Hull (01482) 445416. **Kingston Cycles**, 245 Hessle Rd, Hull (01482) 328832. **The Cycle Shop**, 59 Southgate, Hornsea (01964) 532650.

Docks Museum, Hull town centre (section 10)

FOR ACCOMMODATION SYMBOLS KEY SEE INSIDE COVER

TRANS PENNINE TRAIL LANDMARKS

Since its inception the number of sculptures reflecting the local history and environment along the trail has steadily increased. Similarly new Millennium projects have also added an extra dimension to the trail. Alongside existing landmarks such as the Humber Bridge they make your trail ride an unforgettable experience.

Right: Sculpture reflecting the local history of the Selby area. Found on the Selby Canal, North Yorkshire. (section 7)

Below: Four Winds sculpture near Thwaite Mills on the section heading into Leeds. The standing stones have faces of the North, South, East and West Winds carved in them. (section 6)

The Deep sealife centre is a stunning new addition to Hull's skyline. (section 10)

TRANS PENNINE TRAIL LANDMARKS

The Peace Gardens and Winter Gardens at the heart of the new Sheffield (section 6)

Left & above: The iconic Sea Mark sculpture at the start of the trail on Southport seafront means you can immediately get your bearings. The top of this eye-catching sculpture moves in the wind! (section 1)

TRANS PENNINE TRAIL LANDMARKS

Below: Another striking trail artwork on Southport seafront - The Shoal of Fish (section 1)

The Humber bridge, seen from the route along the foreshore, greets your arrival in Hull. (section 10)

TRANS PENNINE TRAIL LANDMARKS

This fine gateway on the trail near Methley (designed by local schoolchildren) speaks for itself (section 6)

Boating at Hornsea Mere (section 10)

TPT monument plaque, trail end, Hornsea. Check how far you have come! (section 10)

HULL ATTRACTIONS (Map numbers refer to entries below)

• Hull sits on a spectacular river confluence, where the **River Hull** joins the **River Humber.** Its official title was granted in 1299 when Edward I gave a charter to the port and it became Kinges town upon Hull. This evolved to Kingston upon Hull.

• Take a stroll alongside the **River Hull**, lined with old warehouses and still home to river barges and coasters. It meets the Humber at an unusual looking **tidal barrier**, which protects the centre from flooding in the event of a tidal surge.

The Deep (10) Visitor attraction based on the story of the World's Oceans, with stunning aquaria and the latest interactive displays. Dramatic, iconic building thrusts 30metres over the Humber Estuary. Pedestrian and cycle bridge link to the old town. Next to the TPT. (01482) 381000.

• **Wilberforce House (2)** on the High Street is the birthplace of the famous anti-slave trade campaigner. It is now a museum to his memory and has relics of the cruel business he helped ban, such as leg-irons, whips and chains. His **statue** stands on top of a Doric column overlooking Queens Gardens.

• The **Old Town** sits between the old dock area and the River Hull and has a fascinating blend of ancient and modern architecture. It is surprising any pre-1945 buildings survive as the city was smashed by the Luftwaffe during WWII; 7,000 of its citizens died and 92% of its houses suffered bomb damage. Its most famous street is the **Land of Green Ginger (5)**. Also look out for the imposing **Holy Trinity Church (6),** the city's most impressive religious building, and **Ye Olde White Hart Inn**, an historic pub.

The **Docks** stretch for some 7 miles along the Humber's north bank and the fishing, cargo handling and passenger ferry industries make it the country's third largest port. **Victoria Pier** is a good shipping observation point. The original 18th century dock has been filled in and is now **Queens Gardens**, decorated with flower beds like many other open spaces in the city. **Princes Quay** houses a futuristic shopping centre. The **Docks Museum (8)** covers centuries of maritime history, including whaling voyages to Spitsbergen and the art scrimshaw (sailors' delicate whalebone carvings). Britain's last sidewinder trawler, **The Arctic Corsair (1),** is moored on the River Hull and is open to the public (admission fee) whilst the **Spurn Lightship (7),** once a navigation aid on the Humber Estuary, is found in Hull Marina.

Other museums and galleries include: **Ferens Art Gallery (9)**, with a range of paintings from old masters to contemporary art and the **Streetlife Transport Museum (3). The Hull & East Riding Museum (4)** traces the history, geology, archaeology and natural history of the area. **(2),(3),(4),(8)** and **(9)** are open daily and admission is free. (01482) 223559 (tourist office). The **Yorkshire Water Museum**, Springhead Av. Willerby Rd. (01482) 652283. The star is the beam engine. Fri to Sunday 1pm to 5pm.

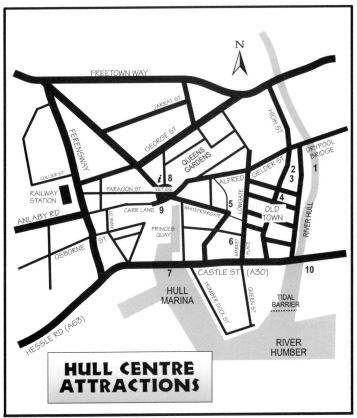

HULL CENTRE ATTRACTIONS

N

FREETOWN WAY

JARRAT ST

GEORGE ST

FERENSWAY

HIGH ST

QUEENS GARDENS

COLLIER ST

DRYPOOL BRIDGE

RAILWAY STATION

PARAGON ST

i 8

VICT SQ.

ALFRED

GELDER ST

2
3

1

ANLABY RD

CARR LANE 9

ANNE ST

LONGATE

5

WHITEFRIARGATE

OLD TOWN

4

RIVER HULL

PRINCES QUAY

OSBORNE ST

6

MARKET PLACE

7

CASTLE ST (A30)

10

HULL MARINA

HUMBER DOCK ST

QUEEN ST

TIDAL BARRIER

HESSLE RD (A63)

RIVER HUMBER

Barges on the River Hull (section 10)

WHAT'S NEW ON THE TPT

MILLENNIUM ATTRACTIONS AND OTHER VISITOR ATTRACTIONS

The Trans Pennine Trail has a large number of Millennium Commission funded attractions along its length with something to interest everyone. Although some existed prior to the building of the TPT many have been expanded and had new attractions and facilities added since the TPT's launch. There are also plenty of brand new multimillion pound attractions such as the hugely popular The Deep sealife centre in Hull and the complete regeneration of Sheffield city centre.

National Wildflower Centre A national treasure trove of wildflowers. Based around a 150m long wall there is a cafe and visitor centre that complement the wild flower displays. Open Wednesdays only (0151) 7371819 **www.nwc.org.uk**

Sheffield Heart of the City Project Heavily bombed in WWII and not traditionally known as one the north's most attractive cities Sheffield is now a revelation to those who visit. Alongside the historic buildings such as Cutlers Hall and the atmospheric canal basin with its pavement cafe atmosphere an impressive and strongly individual town centre has sprung up. The centre of this is the **Winter Gardens**, a brand new greenhouse of a public space full of exotic tropical plants (to open by the end of 2002). The arched timber frame is covered by a 'skin' of glass which actually slides across the surface when the building expands or contracts due to temperature change! The newly constructed **Millennium Galleries** are an eclectic collection made up of various parts including a craft and design gallery, a metalwork gallery and the Ruskin Gallery based on the ideas of eminent Victorian John Ruskin, containing paintings, drawings and minerals. (0114) 2782600. **www.sheffieldgalleries.org.uk** Finally the **Peace Gardens** have been totally relandscaped and the little loved 'egg-box' council offices removed to create an open public space.

A new northern icon - the Winter Gardens, Sheffield (section 5)

The Earth Centre Since its initial launch this environment-based site has greatly expanded its range of attractions. The original galleries built into the hillside remain but you can also take a look at 370 acres of country park, the terraced gardens, the sensory walk and the climbing tower amongst other things. You can even go for a cruise on the River Don. Visiting cyclists tripping along the TPT might be interested in the multi person Octo bike that you can book in advance. You can simply stop for a coffee or a bite (lots of organic and vegetarian food) or you can even stay the night (see pages 32 and 34 for accommodation details). (01709) 513933 **www.earthcentre.org.uk   Entry charge**

Magna   A new science adventure centre based in the huge building that was once Templeborough steel works near Rotherham. Lots of interactive science based displays based around four zones, air, earth, fire and water. Walk along the suspended walkway to see the floating airship, stand in a force 9 gale in the wind tunnel, watch as coloured lightening is generated or see the life and death of a tornado. Hours of science fun plus displays on the steel-making history of the plant including the impressive old arc furnace.   (01709) 720002 **www.magnatrust.org.uk   Entry charge**

Marvel at the power of science at Magna, near Rotherham (section 5)

The Deep Very soon after its launch The Deep became hugely popular. Hardly surprising when it offers a fantastical voyage through the world's oceans in stunning surroundings. Here, amongst other things, you can see seven species of shark, visit an arctic ocean floor, get your hands wet in the Discovery Pool or take a glass lift down to the sea floor (01482) 381000   **www.thedeep.co.uk Entry charge**

BEEN THERE, DONE THAT, GOT THE T-SHIRT
T-shirts are available from the Trans Pennine Trail office (see page 9 for full contact details). You can also get stamping cards from them which will allow you to make a record of your journey at certain stop-off points. Details of stamping points en-route are given on pages 84-85. Stamping scheme starts early 2003.

TOURIST INFORMATION OFFICES ALONG THE WAY

Altrincham
20 Stamford New Road
WA14 1EJ   0161 9125931

Barnsley
46 Eldon St
S70 2JL   01226 206757

Chesterfield
Low Pavement
S40 1PB   01246 345777
(Due to move end of 2002 to Rykneld Sq)

Doncaster
Central Library
Waterdale
DN1 3JE   01302 734309

Glossop
The Gatehouse
Victoria St
SK13 8HT   01457 855920

Hornsea
120 Newbegin
HU18 1PB   01964 536404
Seasonal opening

Hull
1 Paragon St
HU1 3NA   01482 223559

Humber Bridge
Humber Bridge Country Park
(01482) 640852

Leeds
The Arcade
City Station
LS1 1PL   0113 2425242
www.leeds.gov.uk

Liverpool
Atlantic Pavillion
Albert Dock
L3 4AE   0906 6806886 / 0151 7095111
Also at Queens Square
www.merseyside.org.uk

Rotherham
Central Library
Walker Place
S65 1JH   01709 835904
www.rotherham.gov.uk/

Runcorn & Widnes
6 Church St
Runcorn
WA7 1LG   01928 576776

Selby
Park St YO8 0AA 01757 703263

Sheffield
1 Tudor Square
S1 2LH   0114 221900

Southport
112 Lord St
PR8 1NY   01704 533333
www.visit-southport.org.uk

Stockport
Graylaw House
Chestergate
SK1 1NH   0161 4744444

Wakefield
Town Hall
Wood St
WF1 2HQ   01924 305000

Warrington
21 Rylands St
WA1 1EJ   01925 442146
www.warrington.gov.uk

York
Exhibition Square
YO1 2HB   01904 621756

CAMPSITES ALONG THE WAY

Willowbank Holiday Home and Touring Park, Coastal Road, Ainsdale, Southport PR8 3ST (01704) 571566. £3.50 per person per night (tents). Open March - early January. Toilets, showers and laundry facilities. Mini-market type shop nearby.

Hollybank Caravan Park, Warburton Bridge Road, Rixton, Warrington WA3 6HU (0161) 7752842. ⬛ 🍴 🚲 🔧 **Dist.** 2 miles. Toilets, showers and small shop.

Lymefield Farm Caravan & Camping Site, Broadbottom, Hyde SK14 6AG (01457) 764094. £5 per tent. **Dist.** Just off the route in Broadbottom, down track to Lymefield visitor centre. Same ownership as nearby nursery with tearoom.

Crowden Camping and Caravanning Club Site, Crowden, Hadfield SK14 1HZ (01457) 866057. From £6.90 per night. Open End of March-September. 45 pitches. Hot showers and toilets. 5 miles to shops in Hadfield so stock up on food. **Dist.** 0.75 miles.

Also camping at **Windy Harbour Farm Hotel**. Call for details - (01457) 853107 **Blackshaw Farm** opposite (01457) 869447. **Dist.** 1.5 miles

Woodland View Caravan Park, 322 Barnsley Road, Hoylandswaine S36 7HA (01226) 761906. £3-4 per unit. Open April-October. **Dist.** 2 miles

Greensprings Touring Park, Rockley Abbey Farm, Rockley Lane, Worsbrough, Barnsley S75 3DS (01226) 288298 💻 www.ukparks.co.uk/greensprings £4.50-7.50 per tent. Open April-October. **Dist.** 2 miles. Cycle hire can be arranged.

The Earth Centre, Doncaster DN12 4EA (01709) 513933. From 2003 there is planned camping provision at £5.00 and bunkhouse accommodation at £10.00. **Dist.** On the trail ⬛ 🍴 Showers and toilets. 🚲 Enquire for secure storage.

There are no **campsites** in the immediate vicinity of the trail in the Wakefield / Leeds area. **Nostell Priory Holiday Park** is 3.5 miles north-east of the Haw Park section and allows camping - (01924) 863938 for more details. The nearest site to Leeds centre is **Roundhay Caravan & Campsite**, 4 miles to the north-east of the centre (0113) 2661850.

Royal Oak Inn, Main Street, Hirst Courtney YO8 8QT (01757) 270633. 24 hour access to toilets. Plenty of pitches. Up to £3 per night. **Dist.** On the route.

Naburn Lock Caravan & Camping Park, Naburn YO19 4RU (01904) 728697 14 tent pitches from £9 March - November. Shop, laundry and showers. 💻 nablock@easynet.co.uk **Dist.** 1 mile.

Chestnut Farm Holiday Park, Acaster Malbis YO23 2UQ (01904) 704676 ★★★★★ 25 tent pitches from £9. April - October. Wide-ranging facilities including shop, laundry, driers and showers. 💻 www.chestnutfarmholidaypark.co.uk **Dist.** approx. 1.5 miles.

Riverside Caravan and Camping Site, Ferry Lane, Bishopthorpe YO2 1SB (01904) 704442. 25 units - phone for details **Dist.** 0.5 miles.

Rowntree Park Caravan Club Site, Terry Avenue, York YO2 1JQ (01904) 658997. Showers, toilets [🚻] 💧 6 tent pitches **Dist.** Nearby trail on your entry to York by the River Ouse. Facilities for disabled.

Hope & Anchor Inn, Blacktoft DN14 7YW (01430) 440441. 4 tent pitches. Hot water, toilets. Pub food available, Weds - Sun, lunchtime & evenings. Next to route.

Spaceyfield Bungalow, Thirtleby HU11 4LL (01482) 817713. £4 per pitch. See page 72 for details of B&B accommodation.

Burton Constable Caravan & Camping Park, Old Lodge, Sproatley HU11 4LN (01964) 562508. ★★★★ Toilets plus showers. 💧 🚲 **Dist.** Approx. 3 miles east of Hornsea Rail Trail, in the lovely grounds of Burton Constable Hall.

Cowden Caravan & Leisure Park, Eelmere Lane, Cowden HU11 4UL (01964) 527393 **R.** [🚻] ✖ **Dist.** 3.5 miles south of Hornsea. March1st - Jan 1st. Shop. No camping in 2002 but available again from March 2003.

HOSTELS ALONG THE WAY

YHA Liverpool International, 25 Tabley Street, Off Wapping, Liverpool L1 8EE 0870 7705924 🖥 liverpool@yha.org.uk £18.50. 🚭 100 beds. Mainly 4-6 bed rooms and 4 doubles (all en-suite) 🍽 🍽 [🚻] 💧 🚲 **Dist.** 0.25 miles. Self-catering facilities.

Crowden Youth Hostel, Crowden-in-Longdendale, Glossop SK13 1HZ 0870 7705784. £9.50 🚭 50 beds - 2 to 6 bedded rooms. 🍽 🍽 💧 🚲 Seasonal opening. Self-catering also available. YHA membership required. **Dist.** 0.25 miles. Note nearest village services are 5 miles away in Hadfield.

Langsett Youth Hostel, Langsett, Stocksbridge S36 4GY 0870 7705912. YHA membership required. For group bookings in advance call 0870 2412314 £8.75 🚭 27 beds in 4,5 and 6 bed dormitories. 💧 🚲 **Dist.** 1.25 miles south of trail, along busy, fast A616 . Official YHA hostel with basic facilities. There is a cafe in the Langsett village and **Waggon and Horses** pub serves food.

York International Youth Hostel, Water End, Clifton, York YO30 6LP 0870 7706102 🖥 york@yha.org.uk / www.yha.org.uk £16 🚭 Dormitories & s/t/tr 🍽 🍽 [🚻] 💧 🚲 Also self-catering, games room, cyber cafe, book exchange and bird watching. **Dist.** 1.25 miles to north of centre.

York Backpackers Hostel, Micklegate House, 88-90 Micklegate, York YO1 6JX (01904) 627720 🖥 www.yorkbackpackers.co.uk Dormitory £11-12 Double £15. **R.** 🚭 135 beds. 🍽 🍽 [🚻] 💧 🚲 ✖ **Dist.** 0.25 miles. Near centre. Self-catering facilities, bar & continental cafe, internet access.

York Youth Hotel, 11/13 Bishophill Senior, York YO1 6EF (01904) 625904

🖥 www.yorkyouthhotel.demon.co.uk From £10 room only📺 ⤴120 beds

🚲 🍲 ▫ 🍷 ✗ Self-catering facilities, games room. **Dist.** 0.25 miles 🚌

Hull International Hostel, 4 Malm Street, Boulevard, Hull HU3 2TF (01482) 216409
£10 shared room £12 single - room only- light breakfast £1   **Dist.** Within 0.5
miles of both walking and cycling routes, just over a mile west of Hull centre.
Self-catering facilities available.

SERVICES FOR HORESERIDERS ALONG THE WAY

The following should provide horse stabling, subject to availability. Please call
in advance.

Brook Cottage, Kay Lane, Lymm WA13 0TN (01925) 755530
For accommodation entry see page 20.
Bollington Hall Farm, Park Lane, Little Bollington, Altrincham WA14 4TJ
(0161) 9281760   For accommodation entry see page 20.
Manchester Equestrian Centre, Torbay Road, Urmston, Manchester M41 9WL
(0161) 7484374 / 0976 353285
Godley Stud, Green Lane, Gee Cross, Hyde SK14 3BD (0161) 3669103.
Hacking not available on TPT. Phone for details.
Blackshaw Farm, Woodhead Road, Glossop (01457) 869447 Grazing for
horses and horse hire. Also spaces for camping and good local B&B contacts.
1.5 miles from the trail.
Hargate Hill Equestrian Centre, Charlesworth, Glossop, SK13 6JL
(01457) 865518
Pikenaze Farm, Woodhead, Glossop SK13 1JD (01457) 861577. Stabling and
grazing. Camping available for horseriders. Evening meal by arrangement. On
the trail.
Rocky's Ranch, Townhead, Dunford Bridge S36 4TG (01226) 767315
Stable and grazing facilities. Pony trekking along the TPT. About 0.25 miles
from the Stanhope Arms - see accommodation entry page 28.
Joy Cooper, Penistone Riding Club, Tanyard Farm, Oxspring
(01226) 765919 Also very helpful if no availability to put you in touch with other
stabling providers in the area.
Mallard House, Finkle Street, Wortley, S35 7DH (0114) 2888031 / 2887743
Stabling, riding school and livery near the trail.
Silkstone Equestrian Centre, Throstle Nest, Silkstone Common (01226)
790422 / 790497. Saddlery shop only (stabling in emergencies only).
Greensprings Touring Park, Rockley Abbey Farm, Rockley Lane, Worsbrough,
Barnsley S75 3DS (01226) 288298   For camping entry see page 34.
Mill Lane Stables, Mill Lane, Brayton, Selby YO8 9LB (01757) 702940
Naburn Grange Riding Centre, Naburn, York YO19 4RU (01904) 728283
Holyrood House, Hull Road, Skirlaugh, Hull HU11 5AE (01964) 562154

Other Services:
Horsebox parking: 4 purpose built bays at the Stanhope Arms west of Penistone.
Churchfields vets are on the trail near Barnsley   24 hour call out (01226) 733333

TRANS PENNINE TRAIL - FACTS, FIGURES AND FAQS

Length - Southport to Hornsea:
Circa 215 miles / 346km
Approximate Distance Climbed:
650m / 2130ft
(Compare to C2C - 3000m / 9840ft approx)
Length: Chesterfield to Leeds:
Circa 62 miles / 100km
Approximate Distance Climbed:
290m / 950ft
Total length of trail available:
350 miles / 560km

Highest Point: Windle Edge - see photo below left. At the eastern edge of the Longdendale Trail on TPT Map1 West. It's 435m or 1427ft high.
How Long will it Take? Most people aim for around 4 or 5 days of cycling for a coast to coast run. A fit OAP wrote us her 4 day trip ranging from 30 to 65 miles a day. With a similar daily mileage Chesterfield - Leeds would be 2 days cycling. Many people add rest/sightseeing days.

How Hard is it? Generally easy gradients, the main exception being the short steep climb up towards Windle Edge which most cyclists have to push. Many sections of easy traffic free trail make it popular with leisure riders and families.

Which direction should I do it in? West to east is most popular so you have the prevailing winds behind you but it's signed both ways.

What kind of cycle should I use? Anything from hardcore mountain bikes to tourers. Traffic-free sections aren't suitable for top end racers. Occasional bumby track sections with mud / puddles.

CYCLE HIRE ALONG THE TRAIL

Withington Cycles, 26 Burton Road, Manchester M20 3EB (0161) 4453492
Longden Valley Cycles, 105 Station Road Hadfield (01457) 854672 Mob.07887 751997 Based at Royston cafe.
Greensprings, Rockley Lane, Worsbrough S75 3DS (01226) 288298

Earth Centre, Denaby Main, Doncaster DN12 4EA (01709) 513933
Rother Valley Country Park (on trail south of Sheffield) (0114) 2471452
TransLink Enterprise, Normanton Youth Centre, Wakefield Road, Normanton WF6 1BB (01924) 302547   Will deliver to TPT.
Bob Trotter, 13 Lord Mayors Walk, York (01904) 622868

TRANS PENNINE TRAIL STAMPING POINTS

SECTION 1

Cookson's Family Restaurant
8 Coronation Walk
Southport
Mike's News
18 Nevill
Southport
Tourist Information Centre
112 Lord Street
Southport
Birkdale Cycles
272 Liverpool Road
Birkdale, Southport
Beechers Sandwich Bar
219 Warbeck Moor
Aintree, Liverpoo
Aviary Cafe
Sefton Park
Liverpool

Tourist Information Centre
Atlantic Pavillion
Atlantic Dock
Liverpool

SECTION 2

The Wellington
Town Lane
Hale
Ferry Tavern
Station Road
Penketh, Warrington
A&B Stores
71 Walsh Road
Latchford, Warrington

Farmers Arms
222 Rushgreen Road
Lymm
Bikes of Lymm
1 Birchbrook Road
Lymm
Rope & Anchor
Paddock Lane off Station Road
Dunham Massey
Altrincham Bike Shak
10 Oakfield Trading Estate
Oakfield Road
Altrincham
Chorlton Water Park
Maitland Avenue
Chorlton

Continued overleaf

Jackson's Boat Pub
Jackson Bridge
Rifle Road
Sale

Chestergate News
146 Chestergate
Stockport

The Hat Museum
Wellington Mill
Wellington Road South
Stockport

Reddish Vale Visitor Centre
Mill Lane
Reddish
Stockport

SECTION 3

The Centurian
Melander Castle Road
Gamesley

Post Office
Station Road
Hadfield

Cafe Royston / Longdendale
Cycle Hire
105 Station Road
Hadfield

Stanhope Arms
Dunford Bridge

SECTION 4

Post Office Tea Rooms
Off Shrewsbury Road
Penistone

Robinson's News
2 St Mary Street
Penistone

Wigfield Farm Cafe
Haverlands Lane
Worsborough

Worsborough Mill
Park Road
Worsborough Bridge

Elsecar heritage Centre
Wath Road
Elsecar

Old Moor Wetland Centre
Old Moor Lane
Off Manvers Way

Post Office
Park Avenue
Wortley

Wortley Arms Hotel
Halifax Road
Wortley

Countess Tea Rooms
Park Avenue
Wortley

Earth Centre
Denaby Main
Doncaster

Boat Inn
Nursery Lane
Sprotbrough

JS Lakhampal Stores
22a Cooke Street
Bentley

SECTION 5

Village News
176 Main Street
Grenoside

Old Red Lion Pub
210 Main Street
Grenoside

Arden News
Upper Millgate
Rotherham

Merrill's Coffee Shop
16 Church Street
Rotherham

High House
Moorgate
Rotherham

Lunch Basket
61 Moorgate
Rotherham

Rother Valley Country Park
Mansfield Road
Sheffield

Mill Pub
Station Road
Brimington
Chesterfield

Tapton Lock Visitor Centre
Lockford Lane
Chesterfield

BJs Pantry
Cavendish Street
Chesterfield

Chesterfield TIC
Low Pavement
Chesterfield
From Nov 2002 Rykneld Square

SECTION 6

Leeds TIC
The Arcade, City Station
Leeds

The Viaduct
11 Briggate
Leeds

Riveresque Sandwich Bar
15 Bridge End
Leeds

Thwaites Mill Museum
Thwaite Lane
Stourton, Leeds

Mickletown Post Office
14 Main Street
Methley

The Millhouse
Stanley Ferry Marina
Wakefield

Kings Arms
Heath Common
Wakefield

Cherry Tree Stores
9-11 Cherry Tree Drive
Walton
Wakefield

Old George Inn
Sykehouse

Roys Grainery
5 Selby Road
Snaith

Selby TIC
Park Street
Selby

Crusty Baker
18 Finkle Street
Selby

Cricketers Arm
Market Place
Selby

West View Stores
Barlby Road
Barlby

SECTION 8

The Marcia
29 Main Street
Bishopthorpe

Sarnies Sandwich Shop
31 George Hudson Street
York

Edward VII
Nunnery Lane
York

Cycle Heaven
2 Bishopthorpe Road
York

SECTION 9

Post Office
44 Bridgegate
Howden

Hope & Anchor
Main Street
Blacktoft

Green Dragon Hotel
1 Cowgate
Welton

SECTION 10

Country Park Inn
Cliff Road
Hessle Foreshore

TIC
1 Paragon Street
Hull

Chapel Street News
3 Chapel Street
Hull

The Minerva
Nelson Street
Hull

The Deep
Hull Foreshore
Hull

Malborough Stores
1 Malborough Avenue
Hornsea

Beach Cafe
Sands lane
Hornsea

Bucket & Spade
14 Marine Drive
Hornsea

Marine Hotel
Seafront
Hornsea

Hornsea TIC
120 Newbegin
Hornsea

INDEX
MAIN SETTLEMENTS ON THE TPT

Help Us Keep Up to Date

New B&Bs, campsites and hostels will no doubt develop along the course of the Trans Pennine Trail. If you come across such places not listed in this guide, or any listings that are no longer in business, please let us know. Write, phone, fax or e-mail us, using the details given at the front of the book. The most helpful communications will get a free guide of their choice; see page 88 for our current range.